Stitchy Kitty
Fuzzy Puppy

60 Motifs to Stitch Everywhere

Ayako Otsuka

INTERWEAVE
interweavestore.com

First published in the United States by:

Interweave Press LLC
201 East Fourth Street
Loveland, CO 80537-5655 USA
interweavestore.com

Printed in Singapore by Star Standard Industries (Pte) Ltd

Library of Congress Cataloging-in-Publication Data
Otsuka, Ayako.
Stitchy kitty fuzzy puppy : 60 motifs to stitch everywhere / Ayako Otsuka.
p. cm.
Includes index.
ISBN 978-1-59668-183-5 (pbk.)
1. Stump work. 2. Sewing. 3. Animals in art. I. Title.
TT778.S75.O87 2009
745.592—dc22
2009013965

10 9 8 7 6 5 4 3 2 1

Introduction

Cats and dogs have always been my closest companions. Even though I've embroidered for years, this is the first time my pets have been my creative muse. Using the raised-stitch techniques of stumpwork, a classic style of embroidery, I have created charming, dimensional embellishments to honor these four-footed friends. At first the designs may seem complicated, but once you have a basic understanding of the "tricks" of embroidery, the techniques come easily.

What do you think? Let's see what clever designs we can create with our favorite pets as guides!

Ayako Otsuka

Contents

Stitch miniature portraits of your adorable family dogs...

mini frames

Dog Mini Frames

Instructions on pages
62–63

Miniature Schnauzer

Dachshund

Shih Tzu

letter rack

Terrier Letter Rack

Instructions on pages 64–65

Scottish Terrier

Wire Fox Terrier

Boston Terrier

Start with stamp-like appliqués of three breeds of terrier, then decorate it with postcards from your travels and other knickknacks.

A Day in the Life of a Cat

Instructions on pages 66–67

big frame

Sharpening their claws, chasing after bugs—your cat's every-day antics are captured in outline stitch on a large frame.

Dogs walking through fields, cats lazing around the house—
capture their best moments on throw pillows.

Cavalier King
Charles Spaniel

Basset Hound

🐾 stitchy kitty fuzzy puppy

cushions

Dog and Cat Cushions

Instructions on pages 68–71

Siamese

Tiger-Striped Cat

cushions

Throw Pillows with Decorative Bands

Instructions on pages 72–75

*Embellish cushions with a simple linen band, decorative edging and terriers,
or with a Persian stitched onto a linen square, anchored by buttons.*

Wire Fox Terrier

*Chinchilla
Persian*

🐾 stitchy kitty fuzzy puppy

Petite Toy Poodle and Kitten Bags

Instructions on pages 76–79

Poodle puppies of various breeds and kittens undisturbed during their afternoon nap—you can take these little totes along anywhere you go.

petite bags

Happy Tails Shopping Bags

Instructions on pages 80–81

A happy dog's wagging tail and the tail of an elegant cat are front and center.

Stumpwork embroidery is the perfect way to illustrate the Poodle's beautiful coat.

Miniature Poodle

Standard Poodle

Poodle Tote Bags

Instructions on pages 82–85

tote bags

Standard Poodle

stitchy kitty fuzzy puppy

Black Cat Pouches

Instructions on pages 86–87

Perched gracefully, ready to pounce in an instant—these feline silhouettes are featured on pastel-striped pouches.

Two spunky terriers with a bright red heart-shaped balloon decorate this zippered pouch. (Note the tiny bone attached to the zipper.)

Terrier Makeup Pouch

Instructions on pages 88–89

makeup pouch

stitchy kitty fuzzy puppy

Bull Terrier
Pencil Case

Instructions on
pages 90–91

pencil case

Bull Terrier

A pencil case for when you want to sketch on the go. Change the size, and it can carry makeup brushes, cosmetics, or other art supplies.

Carry along mementos of your pets while you read! You can even embroider the names of your pets on the matching bookmark.

Golden Retriever

Calico Cat

book jackets & markers

Elegant carrying cases and a drawstring pouch for all your travel essentials—you'll always look forward to arriving at your destination knowing there's a floppy-eared Maltese waiting for you!

Maltese Lingerie Bags

Instructions on pages 94–95

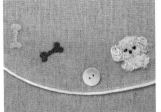

lingerie cases

Terrier Loungewear

Instructions on page 96

Yorkshire Terrier

Yorkshire Terrier

*loungewear,
case & slippers*

Make yourself cozy in this ensemble—the little paw prints of a snuggly terrier leap from the slipper and pad along the hem of the dress.

Paw Print Slippers

Instructions on page 96

Beagle

Beagle Lingerie Bag

Instructions on page 97

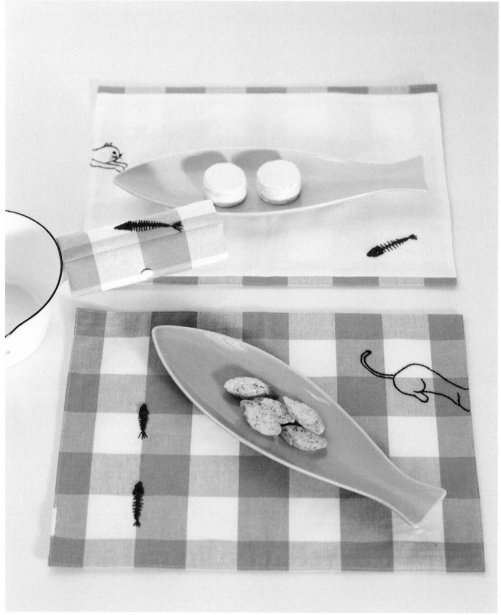

Placemats and Handle Cover

Instructions on page 98

On this reversible placemat, the front and back each show one-half of a cat's outline.
(Isn't he full yet from gobbling up all the fish?)

Chasing after a bouncing ball,
the cat bounds around the table.
The outline stitch gives the
design a simple charm.

Cat Tablecloth

Instructions on page 99

tablecloth

napkins & coasters

Whether you have four cute cats with their backs turned and tails swishing or stylish terriers wearing an array of ribbons, your lunchtime has never been more colorful.

Napkins and Coasters

Instructions on pages 100–101

Dish Towels

Instructions on
pages 102–103

kitchen cloth

*Scottish Terrier with
a bone*

*Calico Cat with a
ladybug*

*Two pets, each playing with their favorite things!
While away a relaxing afternoon, with embroidered
pets brightening your day.*

tea cozy

A charming feature of any teatime, these whimsical cozies will keep your tea warm and your guests smiling.

Tea Cozies

Instructions on page 104

Dachshund

Black Cat with a mouse

pot holder

When handling hot pots and frying pans,
these embroidered pot holders will protect you
from the heat in style.

garçon apron

Terrier Garçon Apron

Instructions on page 106

When you'll be
spending the day
in the kitchen, slip
on one of these
aprons embroidered
with a terrier...
complete with his
meal of choice.

café apron

Wire Fox Terrier

Black Cat Café Apron

Instructions on page 107

From the pocket, a mischievous kitten looks for a tasty treat . . . and meows when he spots one.

Child's T-Shirt

Instructions on page 108

Today, your child can go out on the town with her very own black kitty cat! (What, no animals allowed? Think anyone will notice?)

mother and child matching t-shirts

Adult-Sized T-Shirt

Instructions on page 109

Hmm, the kitty seems to have wandered away, leaving behind a trail of paw prints over the shoulder...

stitchy kitty fuzzy puppy

blouse & skirt

Coordinating Top and Skirt

Instructions on pages 110–111

On the top, a happy Boston terrier eyes his big, tasty treat. On the skirt, a dachshund gazes longingly at the bones, which are tucked in the pocket just out of reach.

One-Piece Dress

Instructions on pages 112–113

A terrier frolicking in a field of flowers meets a bumbling ladybug—a scene straight from a storybook.

Flower and ladybug

Wire Fox Terrier

one-piece dress

child's hat & bag

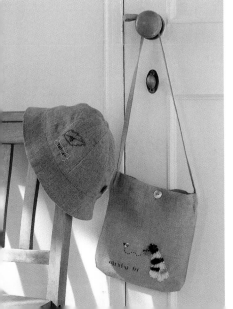

Child's Hat and Bag Set

Instructions on pages 114–115

On the child's bag, the same terrier eyes a bumblebee.
On the hat, a ladybug alights on a leaf.

hat & muffler

The scarf's stripes cleverly evolve into a bookshelf, complete with a stack of books and a napping kitty. The simple lettering on the hat complements the tableau perfectly.

Black Cat Hat
and Scarf

Instructions on
page 116

mittens

Black Cat Mittens

Instructions on page 117

_The embroidery on each mitten is
asymmetrical: when your hands
are side by side, the whole cat
appears._

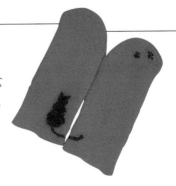

Embroidery Basics and Instructions

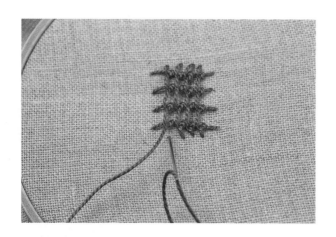

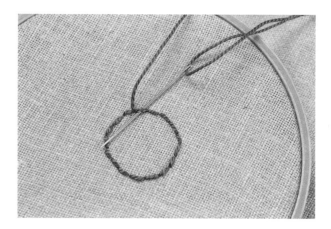

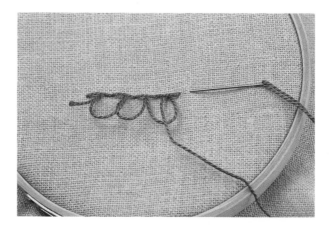

Stitch Sampler

Satin Stitch

Raised Leaf Stitch

Smyrna Stitch

French Knots

Backstitch

Raised Buttonhole Stitch

Outline Stitch

Corded Buttonhole Stitch

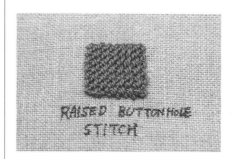

Binding horizontal to vertical threads creates a stitch that resembles woven textile fabric.

Raised Buttonhole Stitch

Stumpwork is a type of solid embroidery dating back to seventeenth-century England. It was used on the clothing and cloth cases of the nobility. Because the stitches are stuffed with felt or cotton, creating a raised solid texture, stumpwork is best suited for simulating the furry coats of cats and dogs. Try the Smyrna stitch, which has its origins in the techniques of knotted carpets, creating furry paws.

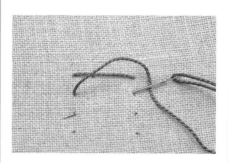

1 Make horizontal stitches the width of the pattern.

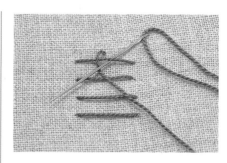

3 Loop the thread vertically around the horizontal thread.

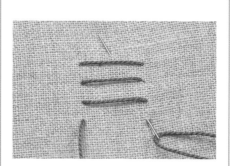

2 Pull the needle out through the center of the first stitch.

4 Repeat Step 3 on the thread below. For each stitch, pull the looped thread upward.

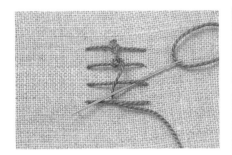

5 Loop your way to the bottom, then fill the right half of the design with vertical loops.

6 Fill the left half in the same manner.

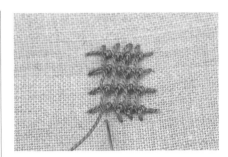

7 Pull the thread through the back and weave it through the interlaced threads to secure it.

As seen in these pieces . . .

PAGE 19
poodle's leg detail

PAGE 33
dog bone detail

By weaving a net and inserting a piece of cotton or felt underneath, this stitch has the feel of raised appliqué.

Corded Buttonhole Stitch

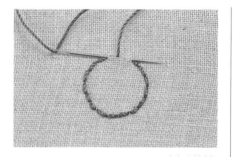

1 Outline the pattern with backstitches.

3 Pull up a loop in the backstitch and begin working the detached buttonhole stitch (see page 59).

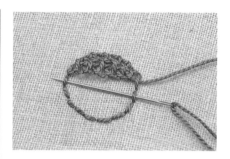

5 Repeating Step 4, continue filling the circle with detached buttonhole stitches.

2 Secure at the top by passing the needle through a loop of the backstitch from outside to inside.

4 Insert the needle from outside the loop on the next row down of the backstitch. Draw the thread across to the opposite side and then through a loop in the backstitch. Using a detached buttonhole stitch, bind the cross thread to the loops of the top row of buttonhole stitches.

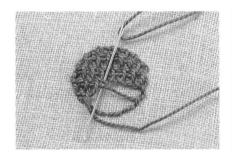

6 When the circle is two-thirds filled, insert a small piece of cut felt.

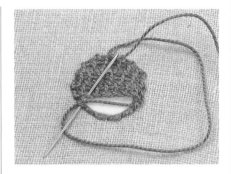

7 Continue with the detached buttonhole stitches until the circle is filled.

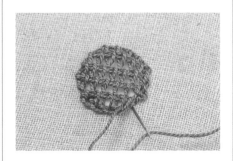

8 To finish, bring the needle through to the back and weave the thread to secure the stitches.

As seen in these pieces . . .

PAGE 11
cat throw pillow

PAGE 33
cat dish towel

PAGE 29
dog on lingerie bag

Using a pin and three base threads, this stitch is made by weaving the threads. It is great for shapes such as ears or leaves.

Raised Leaf Stitch

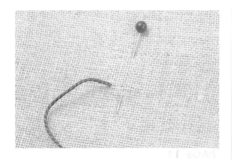

1 Set the pin as a guide and pull the needle and thread out to the left of the pin.

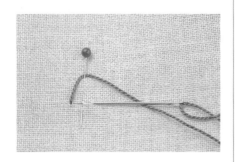

2 Drape the thread over the pin, then insert the needle at the opposite side (aligned with the pin). Pull it out at the center.

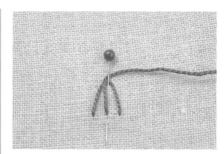

3 Pull the thread to the top and wrap it around the marking needle.

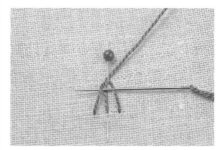

4 Weave the thread through the base threads from right to left.

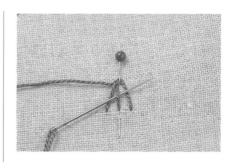

5 Pass the needle under the center thread from the left and draw it across to the right.

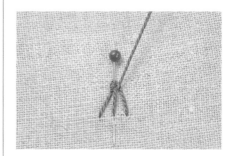

6 Gently pull the thread.

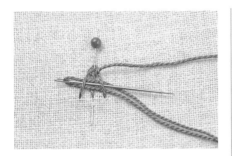

7 Repeat Steps 4–6 the length of the shape.

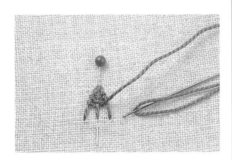

8 Using the tip of the needle, adjust the threads so they line up evenly and maintain the proper shape. Do not let the threads become too loose or too tight.

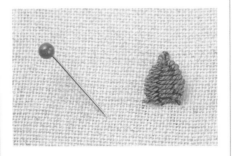

9 Remove the pin and finish the stitch by bringing the needle to the back, where you can tie it off.

As seen in these pieces . . .

PAGE 11

cat cushion

PAGE 43

child's bag

SMYRNA STITCH

A stitch that is developed by making loops. By making the loops longer and cutting the loops, various shapes can be created.

Smyrna Stitch

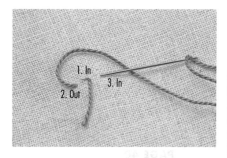

1 Insert the thread at the top of the stitch and bring it back through at half the width of the stitch, then insert the needle at the point of the full stitch and pull it out from the center.

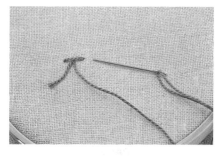

2 Insert the needle at the point of a full stitch, make a loop and come back out at the point of the half stitch (the point of half of the backstitch).

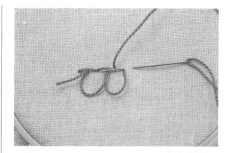

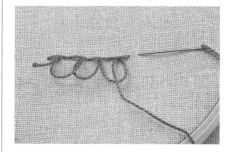

Reverse Side

3 In the same manner, continue on making loops while keeping the length of the loops in order.

As seen in these pieces . . .

PAGE 10

dog cushion

stitch separately and cut

PAGE 10

dog cushion

with a long length cut

PAGE 19

poodle tote bag

with a short length cut

PAGE 40

skirt

leave the loops long

🐾 stitchy kitty fuzzy puppy

Pattern Instructions

Before You Begin

MATERIALS

Some manufactured materials and slightly altered linen tape are used. Try using a variety of applications to create original products.

DESIGNS

Life-size designs are included (enlarge the designs on pages 80–81 as needed).

Copy onto tracing paper, overlap the design with chalk paper on top of the cloth, and using a tracer (a specifically designed pen) or a ball-point pen, trace from above.

THREAD

The thread is an extremely important part of your design. Elements like color and tone allow you to create vividness. There are surprisingly many types of embroidery threads to choose from. It is sometimes even good to try working with wool thread.

NEEDLES

Choosing a needle is important for creating beautiful finishing touches. You should try not to use a thick thread with a thin needle or stitch fine cloth with a thick needle.

PATTERNS

For the materials, except where specified, the numbers used in the design are DMC color codes, and the thread number is marked by the "#" sign.

Where other makers are used, the corresponding color codes appear on page 118.

THREAD TYPES

1 #25: The thinnest thread is 6 strands bundled together. Draw out and trim the necessary amount one at a time for use.

2 #5: A rather thick thread of tightly wound construction, used by taking one strand.

3 #4: A soft-laid yarn, which is called "soft cotton," resembling a soft wool.

4 Appleton: A thin wool embroidery thread that can be a substitute for a fine wool.

5 Tapestry Wool: A relatively tight-bound wool embroidery thread. A rich assortment of these yarns are widely used in canvas work and for other techniques.

6 #8: A thread that is wound tightly into a ball. Pull out and use as-is, one strand at a time.

In addition, there is also a gently twisted thread known as Coton à Broder, which is used as a single strand. This comes in varying thicknesses.

LINEN TAPE TYPES

Linen tape comes in widths from 1 cm to wider than 20 cm, and some may have decorative edging. Linen tape is an optional embellishment for many projects.

STITCHES

Ceylon Stitch

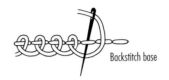

Backstitch base

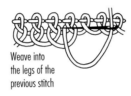

Weave into the legs of the previous stitch

Detached Buttonhole Stitch

Backstitch base

Out

Change direction and go back over

Backstitch

French Knot Stitch

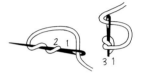

Chain Stitch

Satin Stitch

Out

Out   In

Outline Stitch

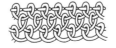

Straight Stitch

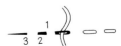

Cat and Dog Linen Accents shown on page 56

FABRIC	Natural Linen
THREADS	#8 Brown (611), Pale Gray (413), Reddish Brown (783), Light Brown (842), Beige (739), Black (310)
	#25 Brown (729), Dark Brown (829), Reddish Brown (783), Gray (844), Charcoal Gray (3371), Pale Gray (413), Natural (840), White (BLANC), Black (310)
NOTIONS	Wooden Bead (1, for the dog's nose)
	Felt (cut circles for corded buttonhole stitches)
TIPS	Stitch the entire body with a felt-corded buttonhole stitch. Add layered details with a Smyrna stitch. Above the dog's eye, leave the Smyrna stitch uncut.

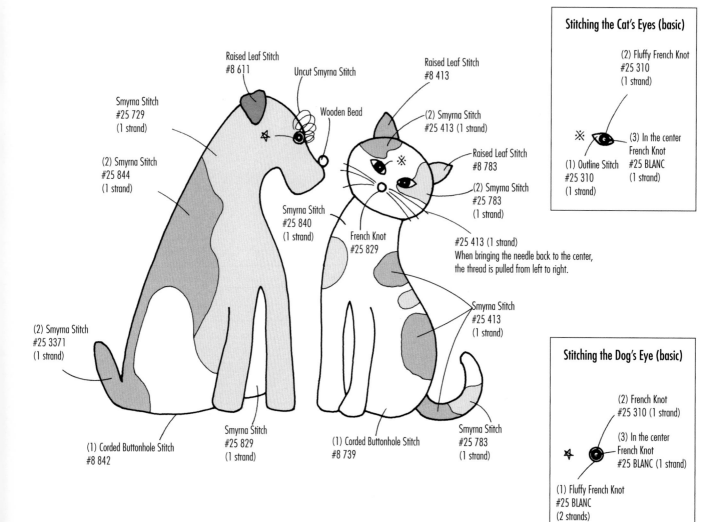

Stitching the Cat's Eyes (basic)

(2) Fluffy French Knot
#25 310
(1 strand)

(3) In the center
French Knot
#25 BLANC
(1 strand)

(1) Outline Stitch
#25 310
(1 strand)

Raised Leaf Stitch
#8 611

Uncut Smyrna Stitch

Wooden Bead

Raised Leaf Stitch
#8 413

Smyrna Stitch
#25 729
(1 strand)

(2) Smyrna Stitch
#25 844
(1 strand)

(2) Smyrna Stitch
#25 413 (1 strand)

Raised Leaf Stitch
#8 783

(2) Smyrna Stitch
#25 783
(1 strand)

Smyrna Stitch
#25 840
(1 strand)

French Knot
#25 829

#25 413 (1 strand)
When bringing the needle back to the center,
the thread is pulled from left to right.

Smyrna Stitch
#25 413
(1 strand)

(2) Smyrna Stitch
#25 3371
(1 strand)

Smyrna Stitch
#25 829
(1 strand)

(1) Corded Buttonhole Stitch
#8 842

(1) Corded Buttonhole Stitch
#8 739

Smyrna Stitch
#25 783
(1 strand)

Stitching the Dog's Eye (basic)

(2) French Knot
#25 310 (1 strand)

(3) In the center
French Knot
#25 BLANC (1 strand)

(1) Fluffy French Knot
#25 BLANC
(2 strands)

Cat and Dog Linen Accents   shown on page 57

FABRIC	Natural Linen
THREADS	#8 Sand (3033), Red (920), Chocolate Brown (898), Dark Brown (938)
NOTIONS	Silver Round Bead (1, for the fish)
	Felt (cut circles for corded buttonhole stitches)
TIPS	Create the fish's head with raised buttonhole stitches aligned in one direction. Then sew one bone at a time, starting at the head on one side of the spine, working to the tail, then back to the head on the other side.

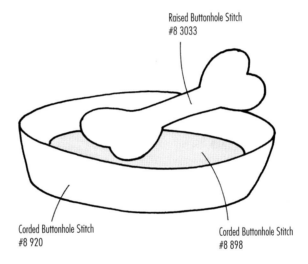

Raised Buttonhole Stitch
#8 3033

Corded Buttonhole Stitch
#8 920

Corded Buttonhole Stitch
#8 898

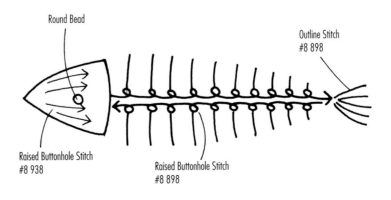

Round Bead

Outline Stitch
#8 898

Raised Buttonhole Stitch
#8 938

Raised Buttonhole Stitch
#8 898

Dog Mini Frames   shown on pages 6–7

SHIH TZU

FABRIC	Linen 10" x 10" (25 x 25 cm)	
THREADS	#25	Charcoal Gray (3371)
	#4	Brown (2642), Natural (ECRU)
NOTIONS	Red Round Beads (6, for the ear decorations)	
	Black Round Beads (3, for the eyes and nose)	
TIPS	Stitch the entire body with a Smyrna stitch. Prick the thread to add texture to the fur. Sew the ears with long stitches, then cut.	

DACHSHUND

FABRIC	Linen 10" x 10" (25 x 25 cm)	
THREADS	#8	Brown (801)
	#25	Dark Brown (838), Charcoal Gray (3371), Black (310), White (BLANC)
	Extra-Fine Wool for sweater detail	
NOTIONS	Black Round Bead (1, for the nose)	
	Felt (cut circles for corded buttonhole stitches)	
TIPS	Chain-stitch from the top of the buttonhole stitch to the bottom, leaving one side of the stitch open for a Ceylon stitch (see page 59).	

MINIATURE SCHNAUZER

FABRIC	Linen 10" x 10" (25 x 25 cm)	
THREADS	#8	Pale Gray (413)
	#25	Charcoal Gray (3371), Pale Gray (413), Natural (ECRU), White (BLANC), Dark Gray (3799)
NOTIONS	Black Round Bead (1, for the nose)	
TIPS	Add detail around the mouth and above the eyes with an uncut Smyrna stitch.	

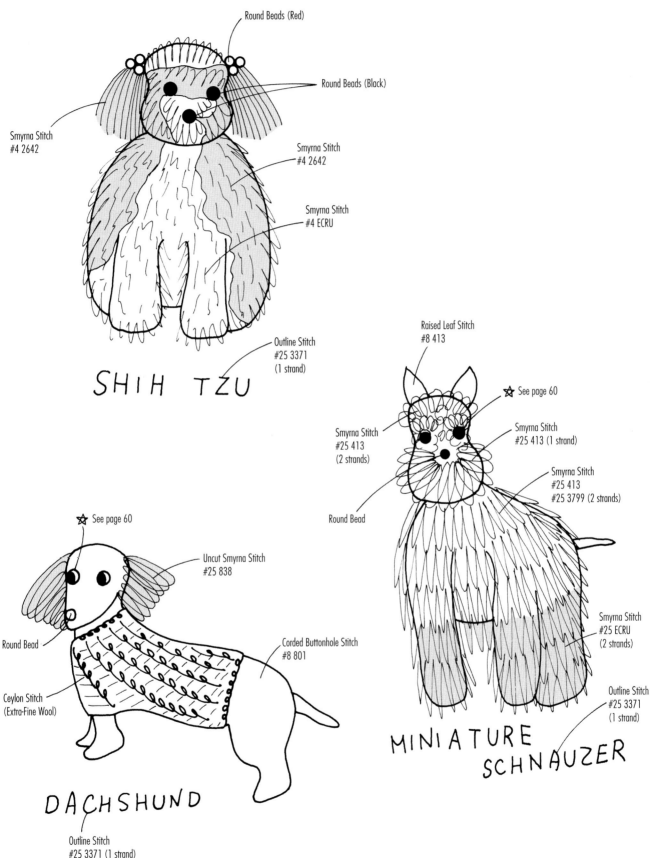

Round Beads (Red)

Round Beads (Black)

Smyrna Stitch
#4 2642

Smyrna Stitch
#4 2642

Smyrna Stitch
#4 ECRU

Outline Stitch
#25 3371
(1 strand)

SHIH TZU

Raised Leaf Stitch
#8 413

☆ See page 60

Smyrna Stitch
#25 413
(2 strands)

Smyrna Stitch
#25 413 (1 strand)

Smyrna Stitch
#25 413
#25 3799 (2 strands)

Round Bead

Smyrna Stitch
#25 ECRU
(2 strands)

Outline Stitch
#25 3371
(1 strand)

MINIATURE
SCHNAUZER

☆ See page 60

Uncut Smyrna Stitch
#25 838

Round Bead

Corded Buttonhole Stitch
#8 801

Ceylon Stitch
(Extra-Fine Wool)

DACHSHUND

Outline Stitch
#25 3371 (1 strand)

Terrier Letter Rack   shown on page 8

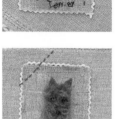

FABRIC	Linen (patches) 3¼" x 3¼" (8 x 8 cm), 3 sheets	
	Linen (contrasting bands) 4¾" x 28" (12 x 70 cm), cut into 3 sheets	
	Linen (main) 8" x 21¼" (20 x 53 cm)	
THREADS	#8	Red (817)
	#25	Charcoal Gray (3371), Black (310), White (BLANC)
	Appleton	Reddish Brown (913), Black (998), White (992)
NOTIONS	Quilt Batting 2½" x 2½" (6 x 6 cm) 3 sheets	
	Rickrack 5 mm wide, 32" (80 cm) long	
	Felt (cut circles for corded buttonhole stitches)	
	Wooden Beads (2, for the noses)	

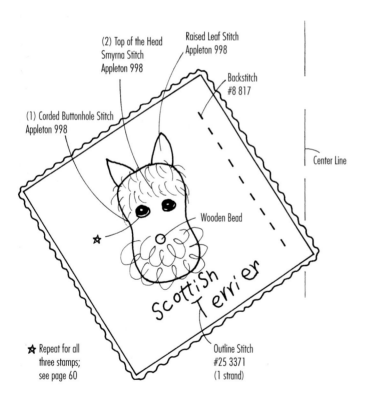

(2) Top of the Head
Smyrna Stitch
Appleton 998

Raised Leaf Stitch
Appleton 998

Backstitch
#8 817

(1) Corded Buttonhole Stitch
Appleton 998

Center Line

Wooden Bead

Scottish Terrier

★ Repeat for all
three stamps;
see page 60

Outline Stitch
#25 3371
(1 strand)

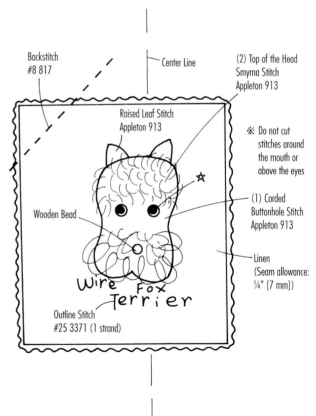

Backstitch
#8 817

Center Line

(2) Top of the Head
Smyrna Stitch
Appleton 913

Raised Leaf Stitch
Appleton 913

※ Do not cut
stitches around
the mouth or
above the eyes

Wooden Bead

(1) Corded
Buttonhole Stitch
Appleton 913

Linen
(Seam allowance:
¼" [7 mm])

Wire Fox Terrier

Outline Stitch
#25 3371 (1 strand)

INSTRUCTIONS

1. Transfer and stitch the designs onto the linen (main fabric, front of the pockets). Layer the quilt batting on the back side of each pocket (centering it and aligning it with the top seam allowance). Sew the rickrack along the edges of the batting.

2. Finish all three pocket pieces as shown in Step 1.

3. At the top and the bottom of the linen band base, overlock the edges, fold them to the back, then sew the seam allowance. Align pockets (from Step 2) on the base and sew along the two sides and the bottom to secure the pockets.

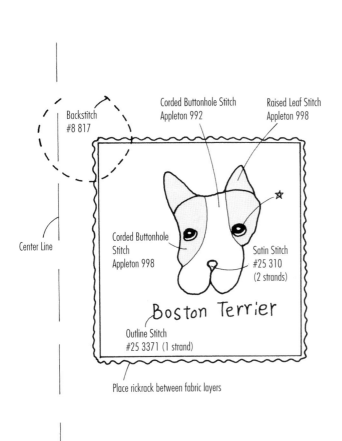

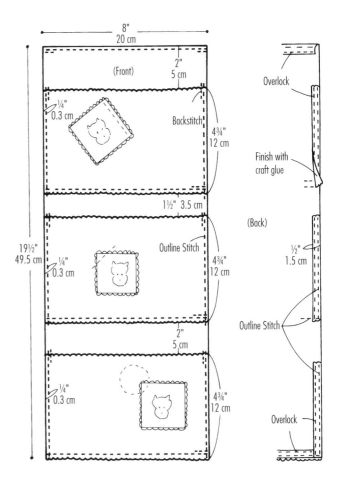

A Day in the Life of a Cat shown on page 9

FABRIC	Linen 20" x 24" (50 x 60 cm)
THREADS	#25 Charcoal Gray (3371), Red (817), Black (310)
TIPS	First choose a frame that you like, then plan the layout of the cat designs within the frame so they are balanced.

Scratching

stretching

sleeping

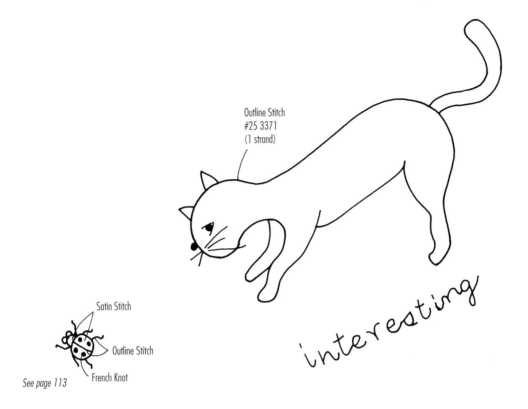

Outline Stitch
#25 3371
(1 strand)

Satin Stitch

Outline Stitch

See page 113   French Knot

interesting

?

Dog and Cat Cushions shown on pages 10–11

FABRIC	Premade Linen Pillowcase	
THREADS	#8	Brown (434)
	#25	Brown (782), Natural (ECRU), Charcoal Gray (3371), Black (310), White (BLANC)
	#16	Coton à Broder (ECRU)
	#4	Green (2012)
NOTIONS	4 mm Black Wooden Bead (1, for the nose)	
TIPS	Using a Smyrna Stitch, stitch the fur details. Leave long loops uncut on the ears and cut long loops on the body and legs.	

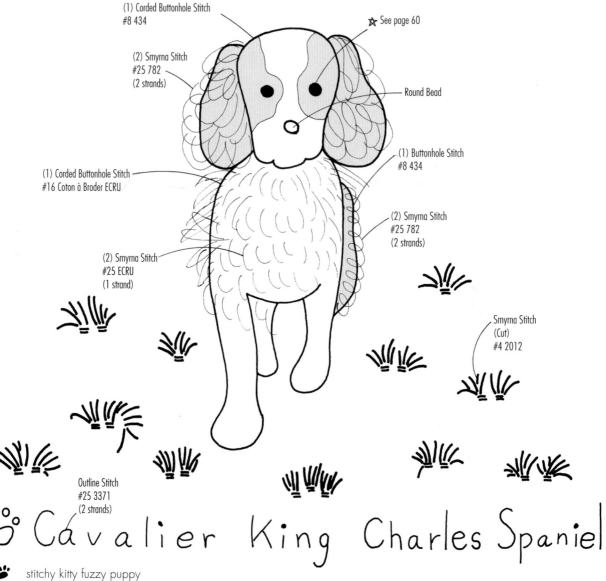

(1) Corded Buttonhole Stitch
#8 434

☆ See page 60

(2) Smyrna Stitch
#25 782
(2 strands)

Round Bead

(1) Corded Buttonhole Stitch
#16 Coton à Broder ECRU

(1) Buttonhole Stitch
#8 434

(2) Smyrna Stitch
#25 782
(2 strands)

(2) Smyrna Stitch
#25 ECRU
(1 strand)

Smyrna Stitch
(Cut)
#4 2012

Outline Stitch
#25 3371
(2 strands)

🐾 Cavalier King Charles Spaniel

FABRIC	Premade Linen Pillowcase		
THREADS	#8	Natural (ECRU), Brown (839)	
	#25	Light Brown (3032), Charcoal Gray (3371)	
	Extra-Fine Wool for yarn		
NOTIONS	Gold Thread		
	Felt (cut circles for corded buttonhole stitches)		
	Wooden Bead (1, for the nose)		
TIPS	Create the body with a corded buttonhole stitch. Working from the top, use an outline stitch to create the cat's striped pattern. Finish with embroidering balls of yarn along the bottom.		

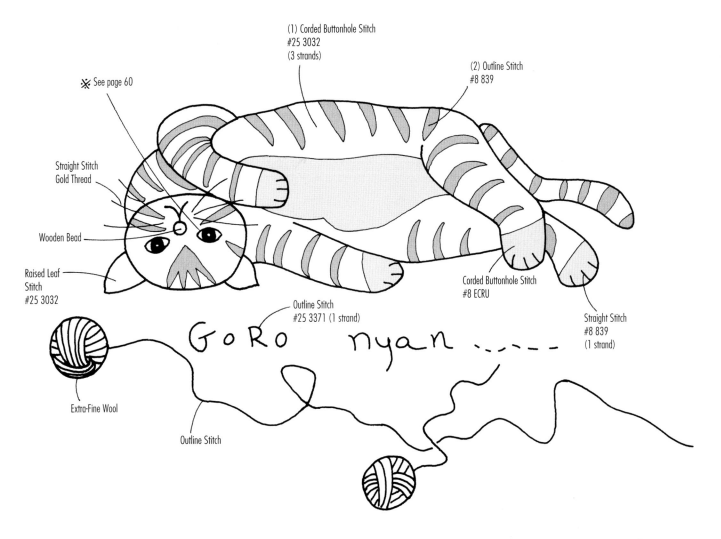

(1) Corded Buttonhole Stitch
#25 3032
(3 strands)

(2) Outline Stitch
#8 839

※ See page 60

Straight Stitch
Gold Thread

Wooden Bead

Raised Leaf
Stitch
#25 3032

Corded Buttonhole Stitch
#8 ECRU

Outline Stitch
#25 3371 (1 strand)

Straight Stitch
#8 839
(1 strand)

GoRo nyan ......

Extra-Fine Wool

Outline Stitch

Dog and Cat Cushions cont. shown on pages 10–11

FABRIC	Premade Linen Pillowcase	
THREADS	#8	Black (310), Brown (433), Natural (ECRU)
	#25	Charcoal Gray (3371)
	#4	Green (2012)
NOTIONS	4 mm Black Round Bead (1, for the nose)	
	Felt (cut circles for corded buttonhole stitches)	
TIPS	Create the body with a corded buttonhole stitch. For shaping the ears, use a detached buttonhole stitch (see page 59).	

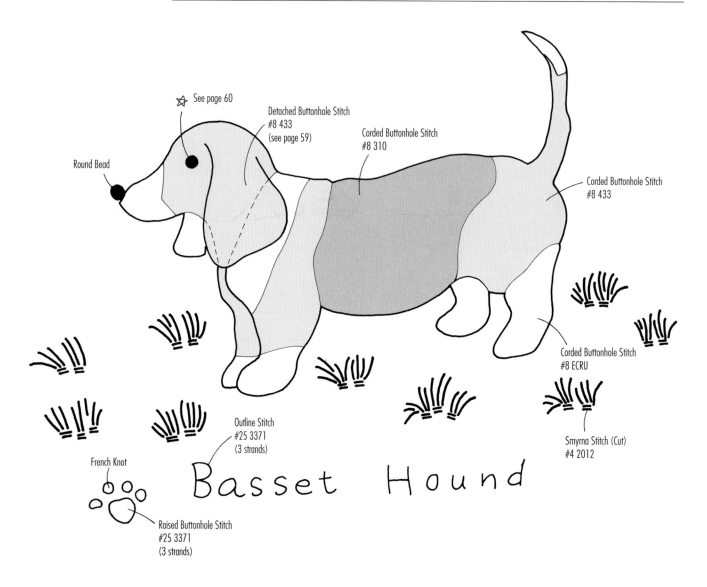

See page 60

Round Bead

Detached Buttonhole Stitch
#8 433
(see page 59)

Corded Buttonhole Stitch
#8 310

Corded Buttonhole Stitch
#8 433

Corded Buttonhole Stitch
#8 ECRU

Smyrna Stitch (Cut)
#4 2012

Outline Stitch
#25 3371
(3 strands)

French Knot

Raised Buttonhole Stitch
#25 3371
(3 strands)

Basset Hound

FABRIC	Premade Linen Pillowcase		
THREADS	#8	Gray (762), Dark Brown (938), Green (702)	
	#25	Charcoal Gray (3371)	
	Extra-Fine Wool for yarn		
NOTIONS	Green Rhinestones (2, for the eyes)		
	Gold Thread		
	Felt (cut circles for corded buttonhole stitches)		
	Wooden Bead (1, for the nose)		
TIPS	Create the body with a corded buttonhole stitch. Attach the eyes and sew the whiskers with gold thread.		

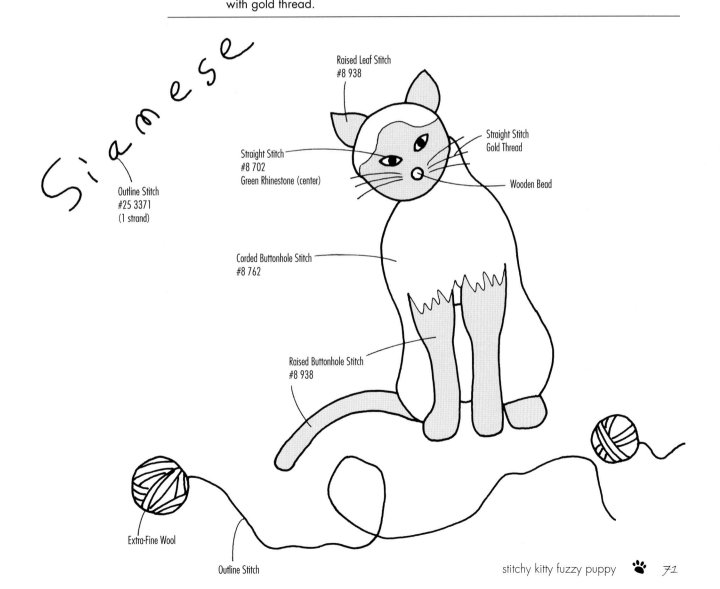

Raised Leaf Stitch
#8 938

Straight Stitch
Gold Thread

Straight Stitch
#8 702
Green Rhinestone (center)

Wooden Bead

Outline Stitch
#25 3371
(1 strand)

Corded Buttonhole Stitch
#8 762

Raised Buttonhole Stitch
#8 938

Extra-Fine Wool

Outline Stitch

Throw Pillows with Decorative Bands   shown on pages 12–13

MATERIAL	Linen (Dark Brown, for pillow) 16¾" x 27¼" (42 x 68 cm)		
	Linen Tape (Light Brown, for band) 4¾" x 16¾" (12 x 42 cm)		
THREADS	#8	Green (943), Red (900), Yellow (744)	
	#25	Black (310), White (BLANC), Charcoal Gray (3371)	
	Appleton	White (166), Brown (183), Gray (963)	
NOTIONS	Wooden Beads (3, for the noses)		
	Felt (cut circles for corded buttonhole stitches)		

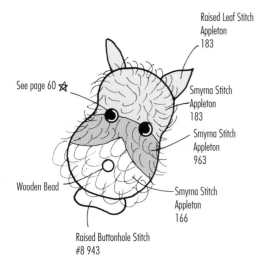

Raised Leaf Stitch
Appleton
183

See page 60 ☆

Smyrna Stitch
Appleton
183

Smyrna Stitch
Appleton
963

Wooden Bead

Smyrna Stitch
Appleton
166

Raised Buttonhole Stitch
#8 943

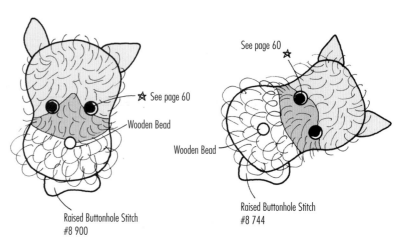

☆ See page 60

Wooden Bead

Raised Buttonhole Stitch
#8 900

See page 60 ☆

Wooden Bead

Raised Buttonhole Stitch
#8 744

Three

Backstitch
#25 3371 (1 strand)

Brothers

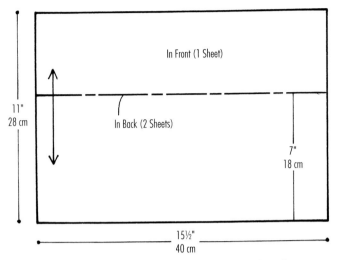

In Front (1 Sheet)

In Back (2 Sheets)

11"
28 cm

7"
18 cm

15½"
40 cm

½" (about 1 cm) seam allowance all around

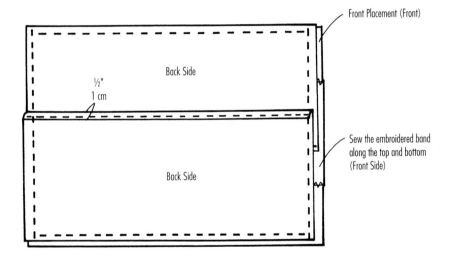

Front Placement (Front)

Back Side

½"
1 cm

Back Side

Sew the embroidered band
along the top and bottom
(Front Side)

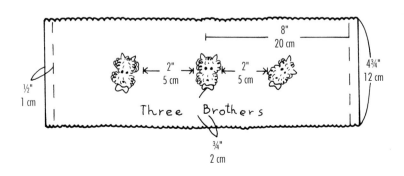

8"
20 cm

4¾"
12 cm

2"
5 cm

2"
5 cm

½"
1 cm

Three Brothers

¾"
2 cm

Throw Pillows with Decorative Bands cont. shown on pages 12–13

MATERIALS		Linen (Natural, for pillow) 12½" x 28½" (31 x 71 cm)
		Premade coaster 6" x 6" (15 x 15 cm)
THREADS	#8	Natural (ECRU)
	#25	Natural (ECRU), Reddish Brown (3859), Charcoal Gray (3371), Black (310)
NOTIONS		Felt (cut circles for corded buttonhole stitches)
TIPS		Embroider the band and the coaster first, then sew them to their fabric bases.

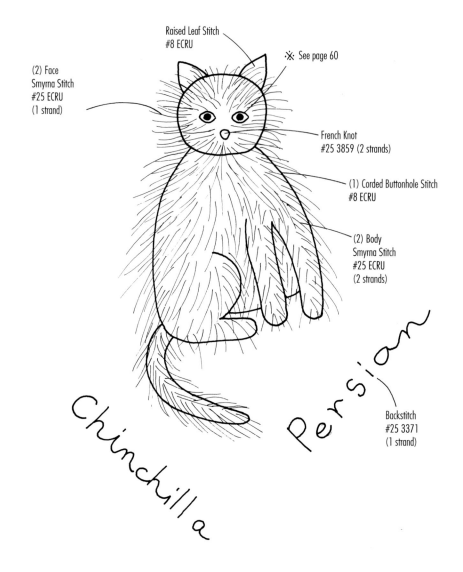

Raised Leaf Stitch
#8 ECRU

☀ See page 60

(2) Face
Smyrna Stitch
#25 ECRU
(1 strand)

French Knot
#25 3859 (2 strands)

(1) Corded Buttonhole Stitch
#8 ECRU

(2) Body
Smyrna Stitch
#25 ECRU
(2 strands)

Backstitch
#25 3371
(1 strand)

Chinchilla

Persian

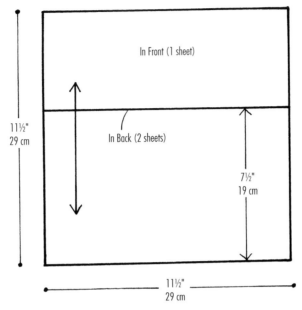

In Front (1 sheet)

11½"
29 cm

In Back (2 sheets)

7½"
19 cm

11½"
29 cm

½" (about 1 cm) seam allowance all around

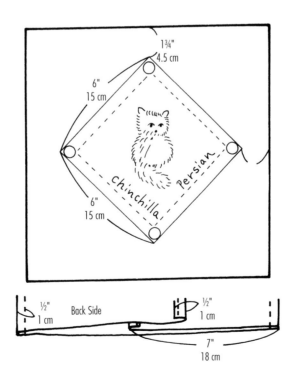

1¾"
4.5 cm

6"
15 cm

chinchilla

Persian

6"
15 cm

Back Side

½"
1 cm

½"
1 cm

7"
18 cm

Petite Toy Poodle and Kitten Bags

shown on pages 14–15

FABRIC	Linen (bag) 8" x 17½" (20 x 44 cm), pattern on page 77
	Brown cloth banding or straps (for the handles) 1" (about 2 cm) wide, 28" (70 cm) long
	Linen (detail) ½" x 4" (about 1 x 10 cm)
THREADS #8	Natural (ECRU), Brick Red (918)
#25	Beige (3865), Brick Red (918), Black (310), White (BLANC)
NOTIONS	Wooden Bead (1, for the nose)
TIPS	For the decorative bands, embroider the letters with a cross-stitch (see page 83). Fold over both edges and sew closed.

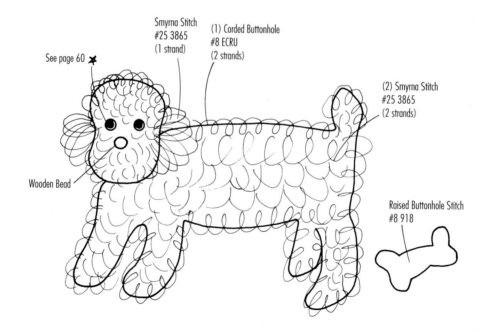

Smyrna Stitch #25 3865 (1 strand)

(1) Corded Buttonhole #8 ECRU (2 strands)

See page 60

(2) Smyrna Stitch #25 3865 (2 strands)

Wooden Bead

Raised Buttonhole Stitch #8 918

Decorative Embroidered Text: Cross-stitch, #25 918 (1 strand)

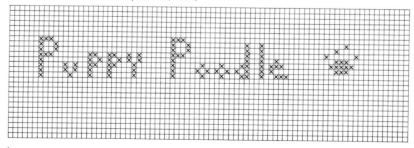

stitchy kitty fuzzy puppy

FABRIC	Linen (bag) 8" x 17½" (20 x 44 cm), pattern below
	Blue cloth banding or straps (for the handles) 1" (about 2 cm) wide, 28" (70 cm) long
	Linen (detail) ½" x 4" (about 1 x 10 cm)
THREADS	#8 Reddish Brown (301), Blue (825)
	#25 Brown (3826), Natural (840), Black (310), White (BLANC)
NOTIONS	Wooden Bead (1, for the nose)
TIPS	For the decorative bands, embroider the letters with a cross-stitch (see page 83). Fold over both edges and sew closed.

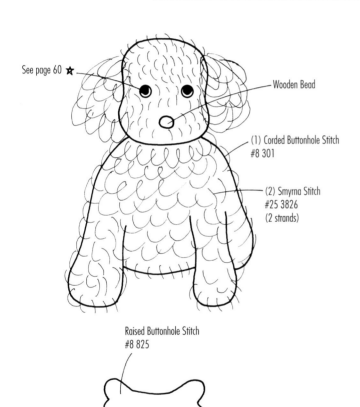

See page 60 ★

Wooden Bead

(1) Corded Buttonhole Stitch
#8 301

(2) Smyrna Stitch
#25 3826
(2 strands)

Raised Buttonhole Stitch
#8 825

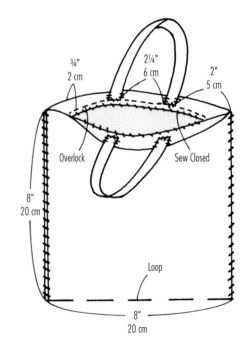

¾"
2 cm

2¼"
6 cm

2"
5 cm

Overlock

Sew Closed

8"
20 cm

Loop

8"
20 cm

Decorative Embroidered Text: Cross-stitch, #25 840 (1 strand)

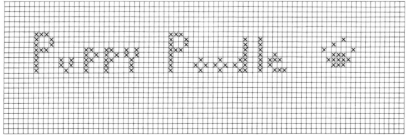

Petite Toy Poodle and Kitten Bags cont. shown on pages 14–15

FABRIC		Linen (bag) 8" x 17½" (20 x 44 cm), pattern on page 77
		Green cloth banding or straps (for the handles) 1" (about 2 cm) wide, 28" (70 cm) long
		Linen (detail) ½" x 4" (about 1 x 10 cm)
THREADS	#8	Yellow-Green (3348), Brown (801), Dark Brown (838)
	#25	Dark Brown (838), Black (310), White (BLANC)
NOTIONS		Wooden Bead (1, for the nose)
TIPS		For the decorative bands, embroider the letters with a cross-stitch (see page 83). Fold over both edges and sew closed.

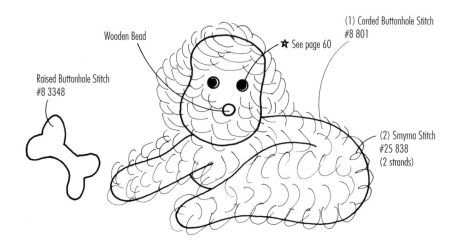

Raised Buttonhole Stitch
#8 3348

Wooden Bead

☆ See page 60

(1) Corded Buttonhole Stitch
#8 801

(2) Smyrna Stitch
#25 838
(2 strands)

Decorative Embroidered Text: Cross-stitch, #25 838 (1 strand)

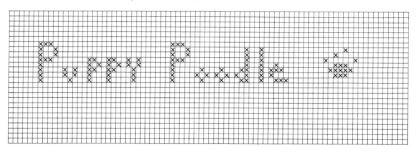

FABRIC	Linen (bag) 8" x 17½" (20 x 44 cm), pattern on page 77
	Brown cloth banding or straps (for the handles) 1" (about 2 cm) wide, 28" (70 cm) long
	Linen (detail) ½" x 4" (about 1 x 10 cm)
THREADS	#8 Golden Brown (436)
	#25 Charcoal Gray (3371)
	Appleton Golden Brown (436)
	Extra-Fine Wool (Variegated Red)
NOTIONS	Black Round Bead (1, for the nose)
	Gold Thread

Outline Stitch
#25 3371

Corded Buttonhole Stitch
#8 436

Ceylon Stitch
Extra-Fine Wool
(Variegated Red)

Raised Leaf Stitch
Appleton 436

Gold Thread

Round Bead

Happy Tails Shopping Bags   shown on pages 16–17

MATERIAL	Small Premade Bag (1)
THREADS	Anchor Tapestry Wool (8196)

MATERIAL	Large premade bag (1)
THREADS	Appleton Black (998)
TIPS	Enlarge the pattern as needed.

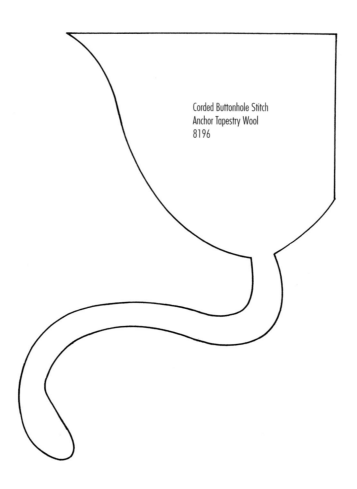

Corded Buttonhole Stitch
Anchor Tapestry Wool
8196

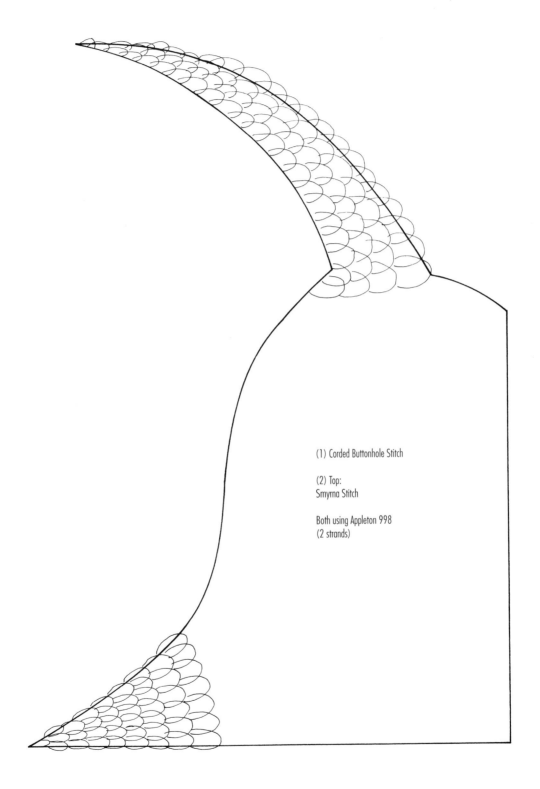

(1) Corded Buttonhole Stitch

(2) Top:
Smyrna Stitch

Both using Appleton 998
(2 strands)

Poodle Tote Bags   shown on pages 18–19

MATERIAL	Linen (Pink, for bag) 20" x 26" (50 x 65 cm)
	Linen (band) 16¾" (42 cm) wide
	Cotton (lining) 16½" x 20¾" (41 x 52 cm)
	Heavyweight fusible interfacing (lining)16½" x 20¾" (41 x 52 cm)
THREADS	#5 Gray (844)
	#25 Dark Gray (3799), Black (310), White (BLANC)
NOTIONS	Wooden Bead (1, for the nose)
	Felt (cut circles for corded buttonhole stitches)
TIPS	Use a raised buttonhole stitch for the face and legs. Use a smyrna stitch to create the head, body, and ankles. Create dense "fur" around the forelocks (bangs) by creating 3–4 layers of stitching. Then, add a vertically oriented satin stitch. For the ear fur, add smyrna stitches in three lengths at ¼" (5 mm) intervals. Cut the leg fur to 1" (about 2 cm).

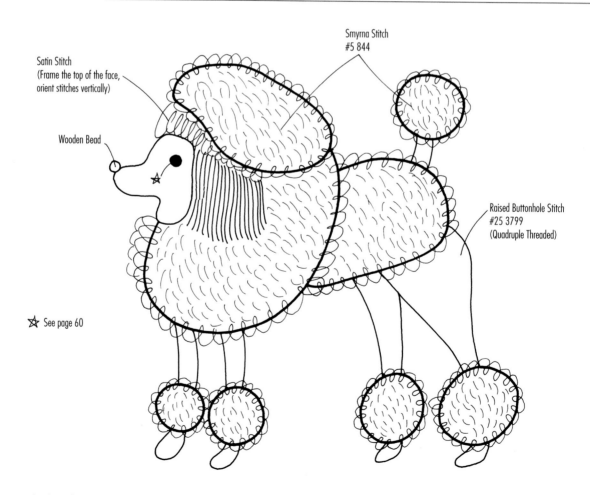

Satin Stitch
(Frame the top of the face,
orient stitches vertically)

Smyrna Stitch
#5 844

Wooden Bead

Raised Buttonhole Stitch
#25 3799
(Quadruple Threaded)

☆ See page 60

FINISHING TIPS FOR THE BAG   Center the embroidery on the front side. With a sewing machine, sew the cross-stitched linen band to the bag's top edge. Finish and tailor the bag according to the pattern.

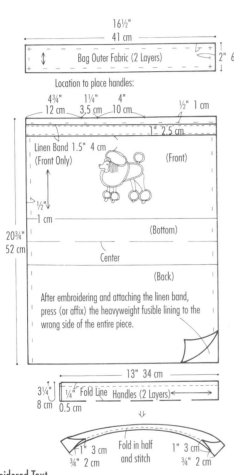

16½"
41 cm

Bag Outer Fabric (2 Layers)   2" 6 cm

Location to place handles:

4¾"   1¼"   4"
12 cm   3,5 cm   10 cm   ½" 1 cm

1" 2.5 cm

Linen Band 1.5" 4 cm
(Front Only)

(Front)

½"
1 cm

(Bottom)

20¾"
52 cm

Center

(Back)

After embroidering and attaching the linen band, press (or affix) the heavyweight fusible lining to the wrong side of the entire piece.

13" 34 cm

3¼"   ¼" Fold Line   Handles (2 Layers)
8 cm   0.5 cm

Fold in half
and stitch
1" 3 cm   1" 3 cm
¾" 2 cm   ¾" 2 cm

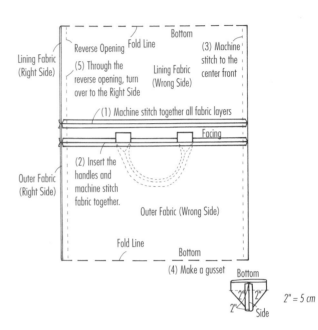

Bottom
Reverse Opening   Fold Line

Lining Fabric
(Right Side)

(5) Through the
reverse opening, turn
over to the Right Side

(3) Machine
stitch to the
center front

Lining Fabric
(Wrong Side)

(1) Machine stitch together all fabric layers

Facing

(2) Insert the
handles and
machine stitch
fabric together.

Outer Fabric
(Right Side)

Outer Fabric (Wrong Side)

Fold Line

Bottom

(4) Make a gusset

Bottom

2" = 5 cm
Side

How to Cross-stitch

Vertical Stitches   Diagonal Stitches   Horizontal Stitches

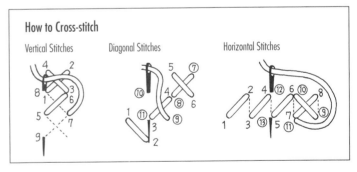

Decorative Embroidered Text

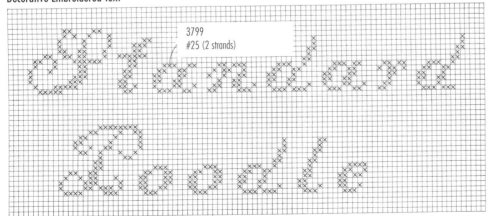

3799
#25 (2 strands)

Poodle Tote Bags cont. shown on pages 18–19

MATERIALS		Outer Fabric: Soft Denim 12" x 25½" (30 x 65 cm)
		Lining Fabric: Cotton Base 10 x 17" (25 x 44 cm)
THREADS	#8	Natural (840)
	#4	Pink (2166)
	#25	Black (310), White (BLANC), Light Pink (948)
NOTIONS		Felt (a few for use as core)
		Wooden Bead (1, for the nose)
TIPS		Stitch using the same points as the Standard Poodle and tailor it to the bag.

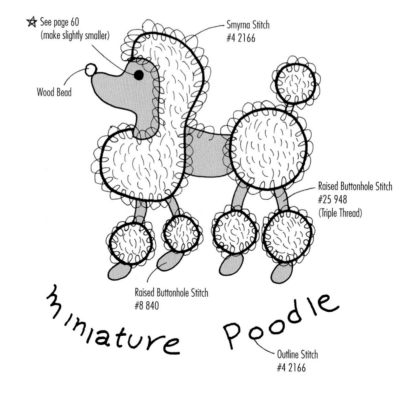

☆ See page 60 (make slightly smaller)

Wood Bead

Smyrna Stitch #4 2166

Raised Buttonhole Stitch #25 948 (Triple Thread)

Raised Buttonhole Stitch #8 840

Outline Stitch #4 2166

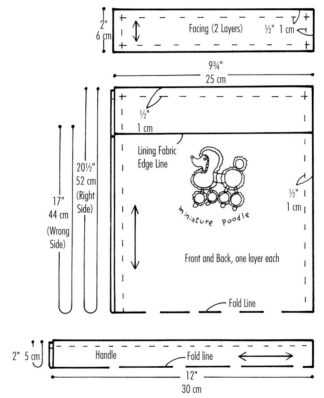

2" 6 cm

Facing (2 Layers)   ½" 1 cm

9¾"
25 cm

½"
1 cm

20½"
52 cm
(Right
Side)

17"
44 cm
(Wrong
Side)

Lining Fabric
Edge Line

½"
1 cm

miniature poodle

Front and Back, one layer each

Fold Line

2" 5 cm

Handle   Fold line

12"
30 cm

Before you stitch, make sure to sew a 1 cm wide band into the center

Black Cat Pouches

shown on pages 20–21

MATERIAL	Cotton (Striped), Blue, Pink, Yellow, 9½" x 22½" (24 x 56 cm) each
THREADS	#8 Black (310)
NOTIONS	Felt (cut circles for corded buttonhole stitches)
	Cotton Rope or Cord, 1" (about 2 cm) thick, 28" (70 cm), (6 strands)
TIPS	Plan the embroidery so it is centered on the front of each bag.

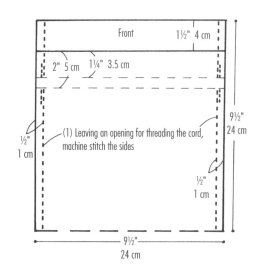

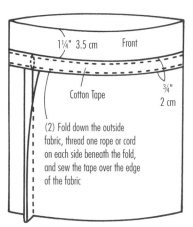

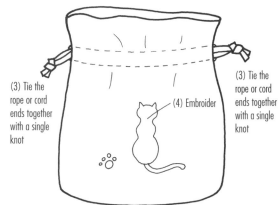

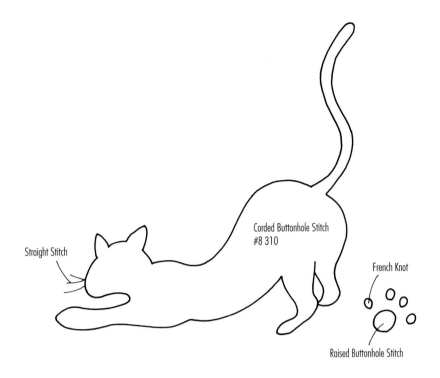

Straight Stitch

Corded Buttonhole Stitch
#8 310

French Knot

Raised Buttonhole Stitch

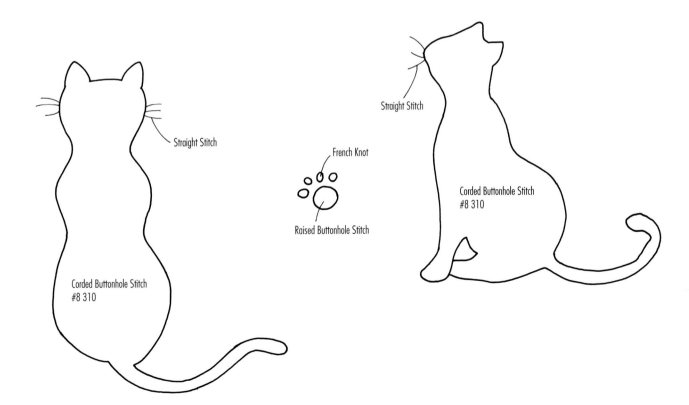

Straight Stitch

Corded Buttonhole Stitch
#8 310

French Knot

Raised Buttonhole Stitch

Straight Stitch

Corded Buttonhole Stitch
#8 310

Terrier Makeup Pouch   shown on page 22

MATERIAL	Linen 10" x 15¼" (25 x 38 cm)		
THREADS	#8	Black (310), Red (817), Natural (ECRU)	
	#25	Black (310), White (BLANC), Dark Gray (3799)	
	#4	Red (2303), Blue (2590)	
NOTIONS	Zipper, 9" long (22 cm)		
	Felt (cut circles for corded buttonhole stitches)		
	Black Round Beads (2, for the noses)		
TIPS	Before sewing the pouch, embroider on the front fabric panel so it is centered. Referring to the pattern, attach the zipper.		

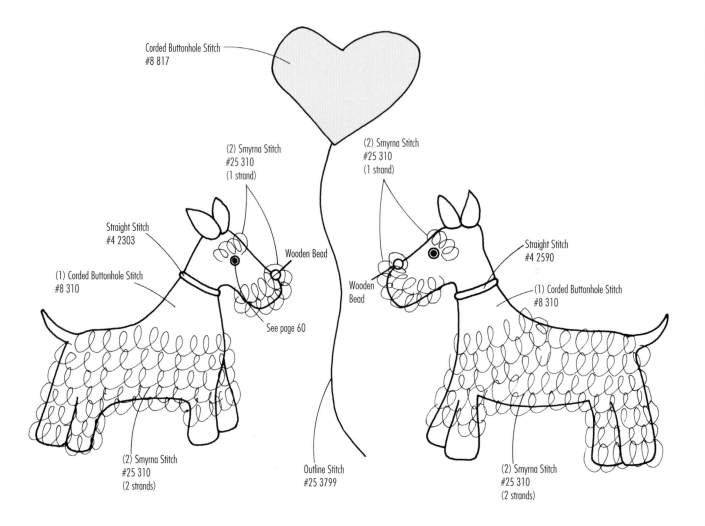

Corded Buttonhole Stitch
#8 817

(2) Smyrna Stitch
#25 310
(1 strand)

(2) Smyrna Stitch
#25 310
(1 strand)

Straight Stitch
#4 2303

Wooden Bead

Straight Stitch
#4 2590

(1) Corded Buttonhole Stitch
#8 310

Wooden
Bead

(1) Corded Buttonhole Stitch
#8 310

See page 60

(2) Smyrna Stitch
#25 310
(2 strands)

Outline Stitch
#25 3799

(2) Smyrna Stitch
#25 310
(2 strands)

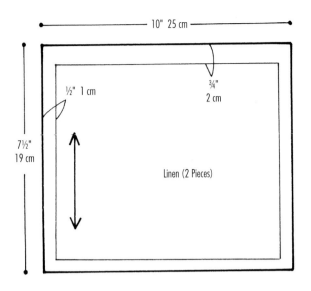

10" 25 cm

7½"
19 cm

½" 1 cm

¾"
2 cm

Linen (2 Pieces)

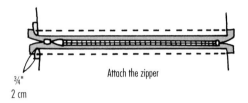

¾"
2 cm

Attach the zipper

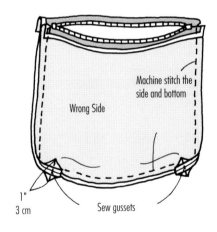

Machine stitch the
side and bottom

Wrong Side

1"
3 cm

Sew gussets

How to Make the Zipper Pull
Use #8 Natural (ECRU) for the thread

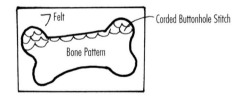

Felt

Corded Buttonhole Stitch

Bone Pattern

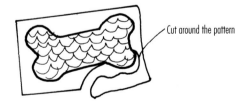

Cut around the pattern

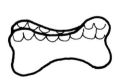

Use a corded
buttonhole stitch on
the reverse side also

Twist two strands of thread
together, pull through the
ornament, and tie it to the
zipper's pull tab

Bull Terrier Pencil Case   shown on page 23

MATERIAL	Linen (band) 6½" x 23¼" (16.5 x 58 cm)		
	Linen (main) 4¾" x 24" (12 x 60 cm)		
	Linen (detail) 2¾" x 2¾" (7 x 7 cm)		
	Grosgrain Ribbon ½" (1 cm) wide, 20" (50 cm) long		
THREADS	#8	Pale Gray (413), Gray (414), Natural (ECRU)	
	#25	Charcoal Gray (3371), Black (310)	
NOTIONS	Quilt Batting (optional)		
	Fringe 3 mm wide, 12" (30 cm) long		
	Felt (cut circles for corded buttonhole stitches)		

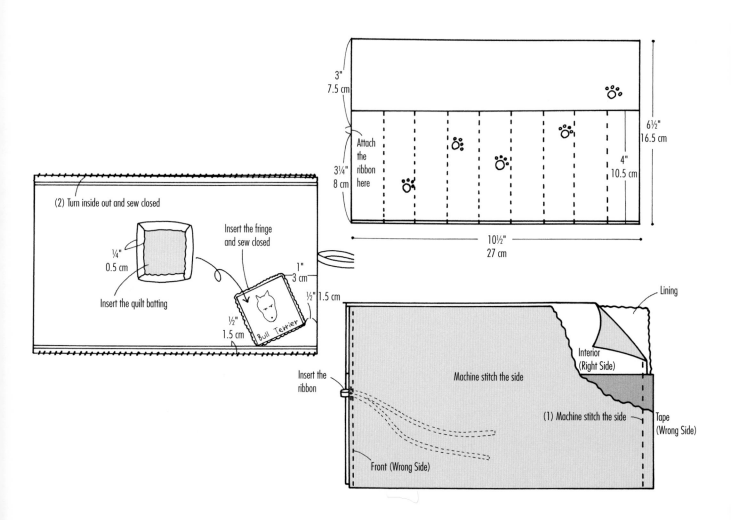

(2) Turn inside out and sew closed

¼"
0.5 cm

Insert the fringe
and sew closed

Insert the quilt batting

1"
3 cm

½" 1.5 cm

½"
1.5 cm

Bull Terrier

3"
7.5 cm

Attach
the
ribbon
here

3¼"
8 cm

6½"
16.5 cm

4"
10.5 cm

10½"
27 cm

Lining

Interior
(Right Side)

Machine stitch the side

(1) Machine stitch the side

Tape
(Wrong Side)

Insert the
ribbon

Front (Wrong Side)

TIPS See page 65 for instructions on creating the embroidery.

Layer the quilt batting, the fabric lining, the linen band, and the main fabric. Machine stitch along the sides, then turn inside out. Sew along the top and bottom.

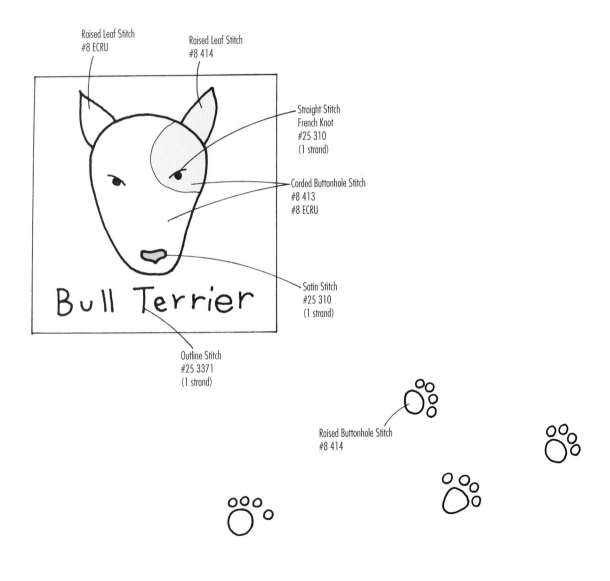

Raised Leaf Stitch
#8 ECRU

Raised Leaf Stitch
#8 414

Straight Stitch
French Knot
#25 310
(1 strand)

Corded Buttonhole Stitch
#8 413
#8 ECRU

Satin Stitch
#25 310
(1 strand)

Bull Terrier

Outline Stitch
#25 3371
(1 strand)

Raised Buttonhole Stitch
#8 414

Book Covers and Bookmarks shown on pages 24–25

MATERIAL	Linen 6½" x 17" (16.5 x 42.5 cm)		
	Grosgrain Ribbon ½" (about 1 cm) wide, 8" (20 cm) wide		
THREADS	#8	Pale Brown (437), Natural (ECRU)	
	#25	Brown (3781), Black (310), White (BLANC)	

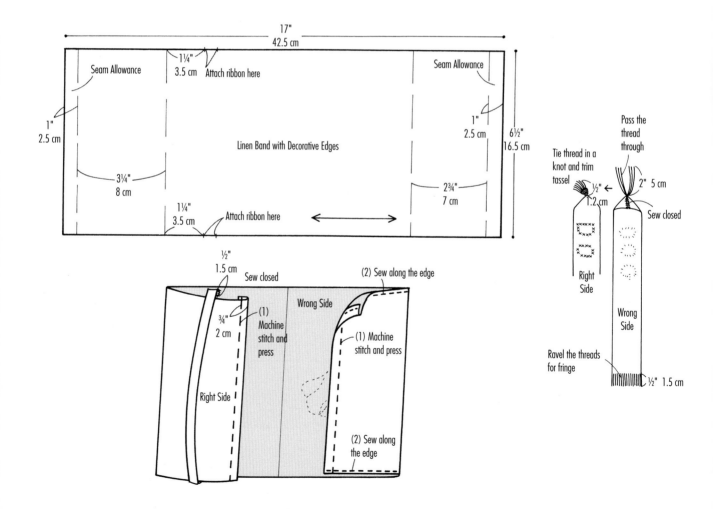

THREADS	#8	Natural (ECRU), Variegated Brown (105), Variegated Gray (53), Blue (517)
	#25	Black (310), White (BLANC)
NOTIONS		Wooden Beads (2, for the noses)
		Felt (cut circles for corded buttonhole stitches)
		Silver Thread
TIPS		Change thread colors when sewing the buttonhole stitches and overlap each color along the margins to add shading.

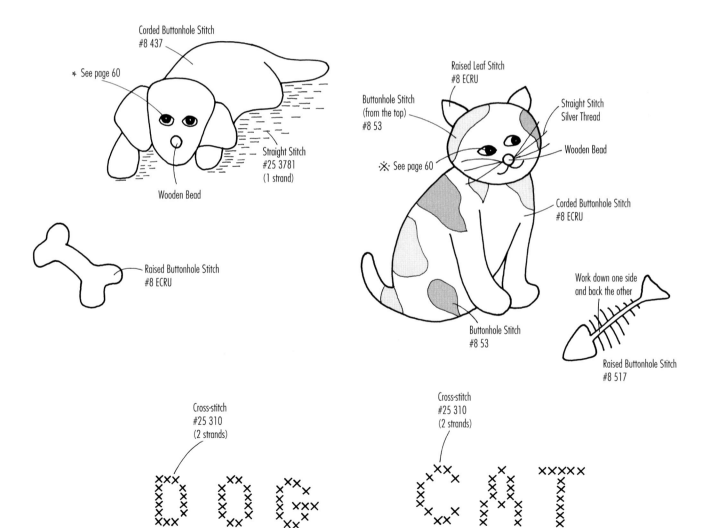

Corded Buttonhole Stitch
#8 437

* See page 60

Straight Stitch
#25 3781
(1 strand)

Wooden Bead

Raised Buttonhole Stitch
#8 ECRU

Raised Leaf Stitch
#8 ECRU

Buttonhole Stitch
(from the top)
#8 53

Straight Stitch
Silver Thread

Wooden Bead

☼ See page 60

Corded Buttonhole Stitch
#8 ECRU

Buttonhole Stitch
#8 53

Work down one side
and back the other

Raised Buttonhole Stitch
#8 517

Cross-stitch
#25 310
(2 strands)

DOG

Cross-stitch
#25 310
(2 strands)

CAT

Maltese Lingerie Bags shown on pages 26–27

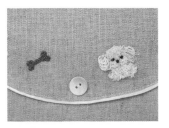

MATERIAL	Premade Lingerie Cases: large, small, pouch	
THREADS	#8	Natural (ECRU), Variegated Green (122), Red (356), Yellow (744), Blue (517)
	#25	Natural (ECRU), Black (310), Green (3346), White (BLANC), Charcoal Gray (3371)
NOTIONS	Wooden Beads (3, for the noses)	
TIPS	All three patterns use the same thread and are sewn in the same way.	
	Place the grass along the bottom of the pouch and scatter the footprints around.	

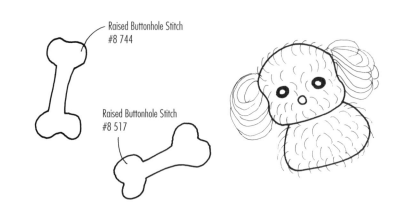

Raised Buttonhole Stitch
#8 744

Raised Buttonhole Stitch
#8 517

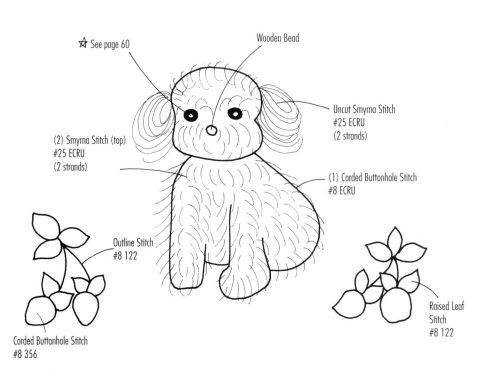

☆ See page 60

Wooden Bead

Uncut Smyrna Stitch
#25 ECRU
(2 strands)

(2) Smyrna Stitch (top)
#25 ECRU
(2 strands)

(1) Corded Buttonhole Stitch
#8 ECRU

Outline Stitch
#8 122

Corded Buttonhole Stitch
#8 356

Raised Leaf
Stitch
#8 122

Left side of pattern:

Corded Buttonhole Stitch
#8 356

Backstitch
#25 3371
(2 strands)

Outline Stitch
#25 3346
(2 strands)

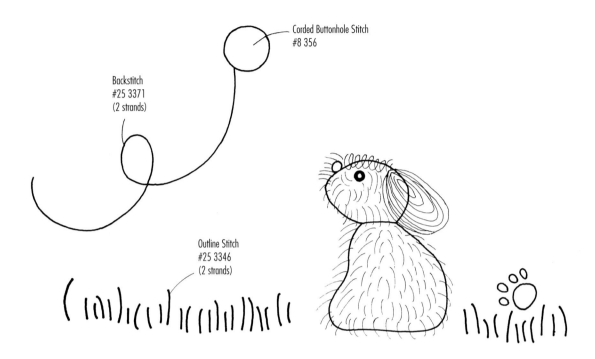

Right side of pattern:

Raised Buttonhole Stitch
#25 3371
(2 strands)

French Knot
#25 3371
(2 strands)

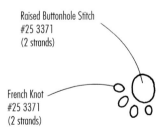

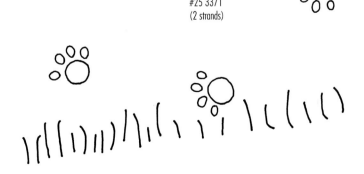

Terrier Loungewear   shown on page 28

MATERIAL	Premade Lounge Wear
THREADS	#8 Reddish Brown (783), Black (310)
	#25 Gray (318), Brown (729), Charcoal Gray (3371), Brown (830), Dark Gray (3799)
NOTIONS	Felt (cut circles for corded buttonhole stitches)
TIPS	Use a smyrna stitch to embroider the face, leaving space around the center for the nose.

The arrows indicate the direction of the smyrna stitch

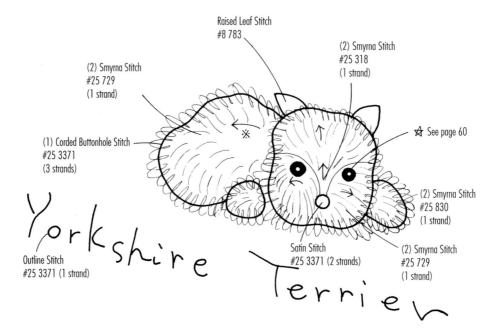

Raised Leaf Stitch
#8 783

(2) Smyrna Stitch
#25 729
(1 strand)

(2) Smyrna Stitch
#25 318
(1 strand)

(1) Corded Buttonhole Stitch
#25 3371
(3 strands)

☆ See page 60

(2) Smyrna Stitch
#25 830
(1 strand)

Outline Stitch
#25 3371 (1 strand)

Satin Stitch
#25 3371 (2 strands)

(2) Smyrna Stitch
#25 729
(1 strand)

Paw Print Slippers   shown on page 29

MATERIAL	Premade Slippers
THREADS	#25 Natural (840)

Raised Buttonhole Stitch
#25 840
(2 strands)

Beagle Lingerie Bag   shown on page 29

MATERIAL	Large Premade Cotton Napkin, Dish Towel, or Other Finished Linen	
	Cotton Tape ¼" x 32" (0.8 x 80 cm)	
THREADS	#8	Natural (840), Black (310), Natural (ECRU)
	#25	Charcoal Gray (3371)
NOTIONS	Felt (cut circles for corded buttonhole stitches)	
	Wooden Bead (1, for the nose)	
TIPS	Use a double-threaded, corded buttonhole stitch	
	Cut the premade large napkin in half. Sew into a circle, machine stitch along the bottom, and tailor into a bag. Sew on the cotton tape.	

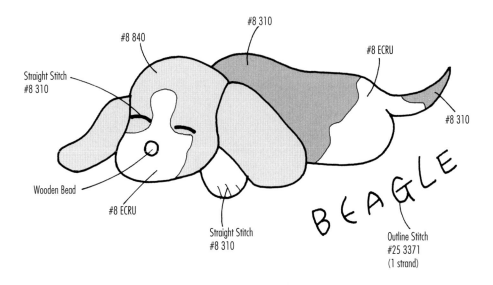

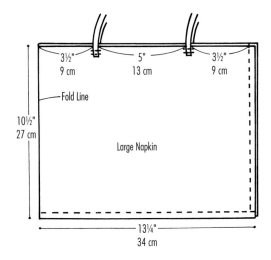

Placemats and Handle Cover   shown on page 30

MATERIAL	Premade Placemats (2) and Handle Cover		
THREADS	#8	Brown (801), Dark Brown (938)	
	#25	Charcoal Gray (3371)	
NOTIONS	Blue Round Bead (1, for the fish eye)		
TIPS	One half of the embroidered design should appear on one placemat and the second half on the other placemat.		

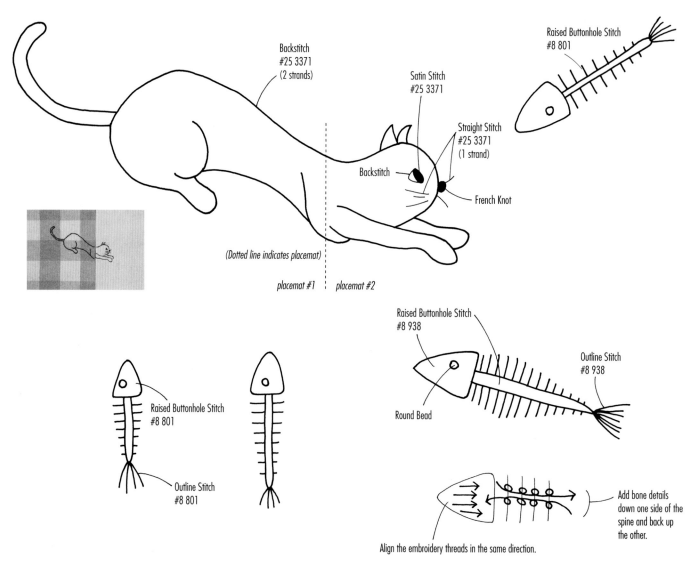

Backstitch
#25 3371
(2 strands)

Raised Buttonhole Stitch
#8 801

Satin Stitch
#25 3371

Straight Stitch
#25 3371
(1 strand)

Backstitch

French Knot

(Dotted line indicates placemat)

placemat #1   placemat #2

Raised Buttonhole Stitch
#8 938

Outline Stitch
#8 938

Round Bead

Raised Buttonhole Stitch
#8 801

Outline Stitch
#8 801

Align the embroidery threads in the same direction.

Add bone details
down one side of the
spine and back up
the other.

Cat Tablecloth   shown on page 31

MATERIAL	Premade Tablecloth (1)
THREADS	#8 Orange (740, 741, 742, 946, 947)
	#25 Brown (801)
TIPS	Refer to the sample layout when planning the embroidery. Enlarge the pattern as needed.

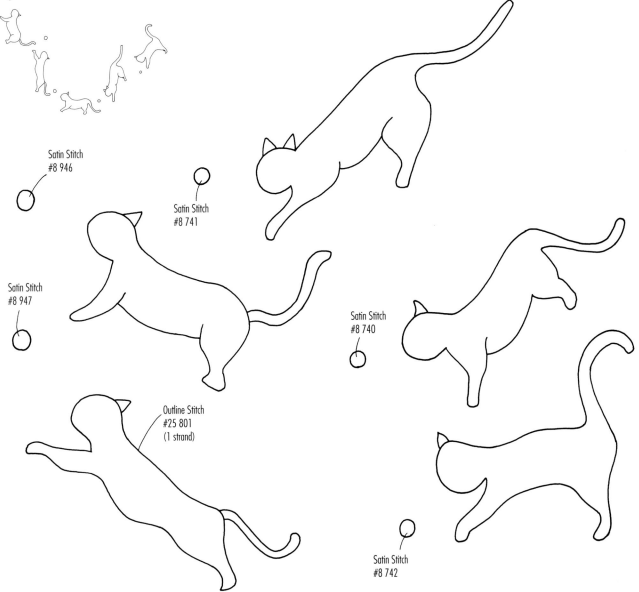

Satin Stitch
#8 946

Satin Stitch
#8 741

Satin Stitch
#8 947

Satin Stitch
#8 740

Outline Stitch
#25 801
(1 strand)

Satin Stitch
#8 742

Napkins and Coasters   shown on page 32

MATERIAL	Premade Napkins and Coasters		
THREADS	#8	Black (310), Orange (740, 741, 947), Green (943), Natural (ECRU), Brown (840)	
	#25	Charcoal Gray (3371)	
NOTIONS	Felt (cut circles for corded buttonhole stitches)		
TIPS	For the pattern sections, embroider a short-looped smyrna stitch. Do not cut the loops.		

Corded Buttonhole Stitch
#8 310

#8 943

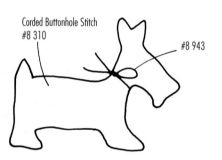

Tie a bow around the neck for each right-facing terrier
#8 741, 740, 947

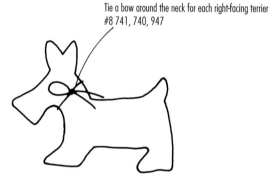

Scottish Terrier

Outline Stitch
#25 3371
(1 strand)

Coaster embroidery pattern

Corded Buttonhole Stitch
#8 840

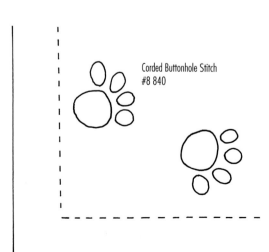

Raised Buttonhole Stitch
#8 ECRU

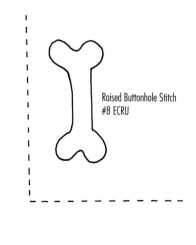

MATERIAL	Premade Napkins and Coasters	
THREADS	#8	Red (900), Dark Brown (938), Yellow (743), Navy Blue (820), Light Green (703)
	#25	Charcoal Gray (3371)
NOTIONS	Felt (cut circles for corded buttonhole stitches)	
TIPS	For the pattern sections, embroider a short-looped smyrna stitch. Do not cut the loops.	

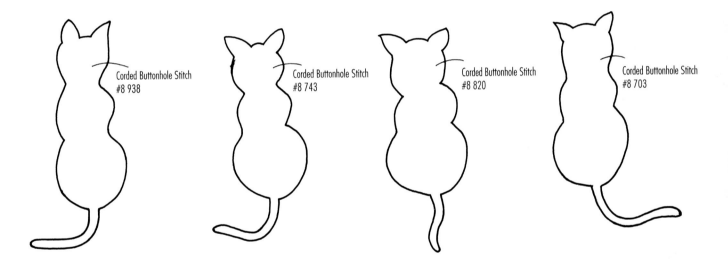

Corded Buttonhole Stitch
#8 938

Corded Buttonhole Stitch
#8 743

Corded Buttonhole Stitch
#8 820

Corded Buttonhole Stitch
#8 703

Cats & mouse

Outline Stitch
#25 3371
(1 strand)

Backstitch
#25 3371

Raised Buttonhole Stitch
#8 900

Dish Towels shown on page 33

MATERIAL	Premade Dish Towel	
THREADS	#8	Natural (ECRU)
	#25	Pale Gray (413), Brown (433), Black (310), Red (817)

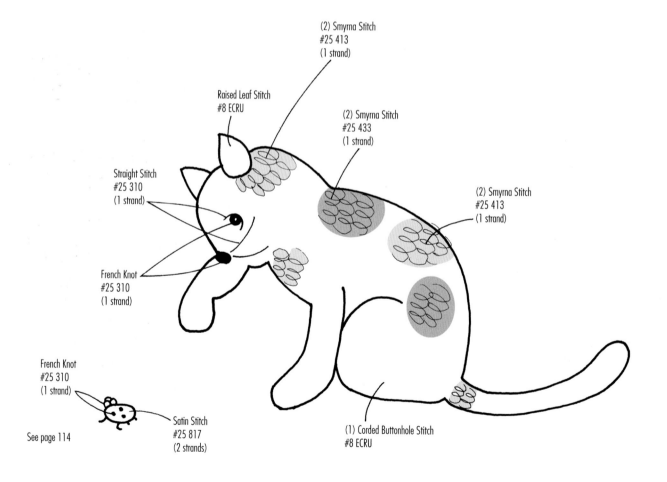

Raised Leaf Stitch
#8 ECRU

(2) Smyrna Stitch
#25 413
(1 strand)

(2) Smyrna Stitch
#25 433
(1 strand)

(2) Smyrna Stitch
#25 413
(1 strand)

Straight Stitch
#25 310
(1 strand)

French Knot
#25 310
(1 strand)

French Knot
#25 310
(1 strand)

Satin Stitch
#25 817
(2 strands)

See page 114

(1) Corded Buttonhole Stitch
#8 ECRU

MATERIAL	Premade Dish Towel
THREADS	#8 Black (310), White (BLANC), Blue (825)
	#25 Black (310), White (BLANC)
NOTIONS	Black Round Beads (1 large for the nose and 2 small for the eyes)
	Yarn (about 6" [15 cm])

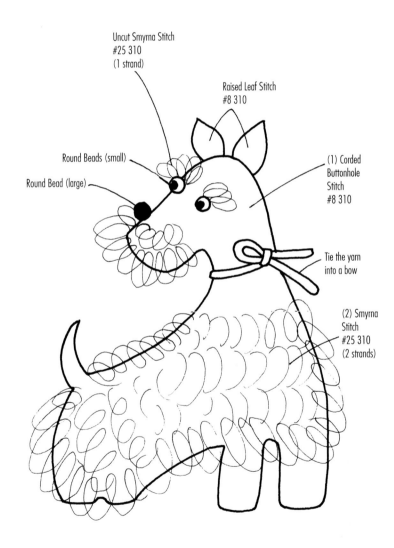

Uncut Smyrna Stitch
#25 310
(1 strand)

Raised Leaf Stitch
#8 310

Round Beads (small)

Round Bead (large)

(1) Corded
Buttonhole
Stitch
#8 310

Tie the yarn
into a bow

(2) Smyrna
Stitch
#25 310
(2 strands)

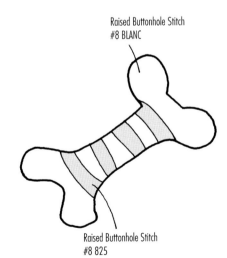

Raised Buttonhole Stitch
#8 BLANC

Raised Buttonhole Stitch
#8 825

Tea Cozies shown on page 34

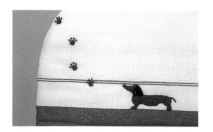

MATERIAL	Premade Tea Cozy	
THREADS	#8	Brown (801)
	#25	Charcoal Gray (3371), White (BLANC)
NOTIONS	3 mm Brown Wooden Bead (1, for the dog's nose)	
	Black Round Bead (1, for the dog's eye)	

MATERIAL	Premade Tea Cozy	
THREADS	#8	Black (310), Red (304)
	#25	Black (310)
NOTIONS	Wooden Bead (1, for the mouse's eye)	
	Silver Thread	

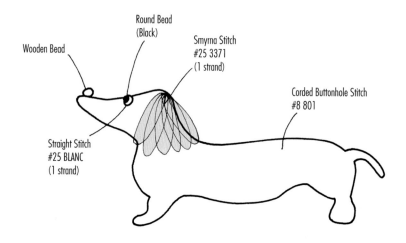

Wooden Bead

Round Bead (Black)

Smyrna Stitch #25 3371 (1 strand)

Corded Buttonhole Stitch #8 801

Straight Stitch #25 BLANC (1 strand)

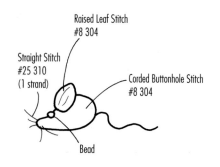

Raised Leaf Stitch #8 304

Straight Stitch #25 310 (1 strand)

Corded Buttonhole Stitch #8 304

Bead

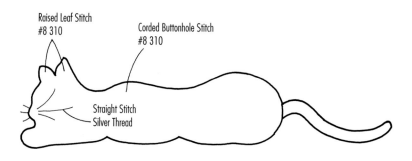

Raised Leaf Stitch #8 310

Corded Buttonhole Stitch #8 310

Straight Stitch Silver Thread

Pot Holders shown on page 35

MATERIAL	Premade Pot Holder
THREADS	#8 Variegated Orange (51), Navy Blue (820), Yellow-Green (907)

MATERIAL	Premade Pot Holder
THREADS	#8 Navy Blue (820)
TIPS	Use raised buttonhole stitch for the head and align all stitches in one direction. Use a raised buttonhole stitch aligned lengthwise for the body and tail.

MATERIAL	Premade Pot Holder
THREADS	#8 Brown (801)

Raised Buttonhole Stitch: After completing one column of stitches, pass the needle and thread to the wrong side then out at the top so you can stitch another column in the same direction

#8 820

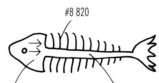

Raised Buttonhole Stitch: Stitches run in one direction

Raised Buttonhole Stitch: Stitches should run top to bottom, then bottom to top

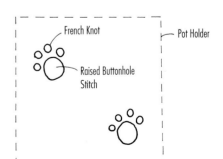

French Knot

Raised Buttonhole Stitch

Pot Holder

Terrier Garçon Apron shown on page 36

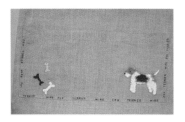

MATERIAL	Premade Waiter's Apron
THREADS	#8 Golden Brown (436), Natural (ECRU), Brown (433), Pale Brown (437)
	#25 Light Brown (435), Dark Gray (3799), Natural (ECRU), White (BLANC), Charcoal Gray (3371)
NOTIONS	Wooden Bead (1, for the nose)

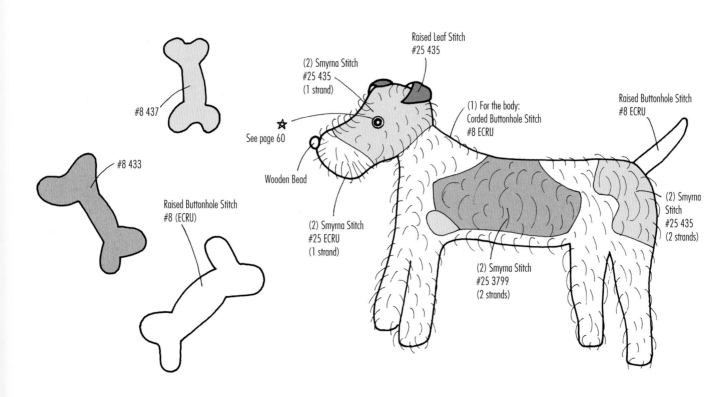

#8 437

#8 433

Raised Buttonhole Stitch
#8 (ECRU)

See page 60

Wooden Bead

(2) Smyrna Stitch
#25 435
(1 strand)

Raised Leaf Stitch
#25 435

(2) Smyrna Stitch
#25 435
(1 strand)

(1) For the body:
Corded Buttonhole Stitch
#8 ECRU

Raised Buttonhole Stitch
#8 ECRU

(2) Smyrna
Stitch
#25 435
(2 strands)

(2) Smyrna Stitch
#25 ECRU
(1 strand)

(2) Smyrna Stitch
#25 3799
(2 strands)

WIRE FOX TERRIER

Outline Stitch
#25 3371
(1 strand)

Black Cat Café Apron   shown on page 37

MATERIAL	Premade Café Apron	
THREADS	#8	Dark Gray (3799)
	#25	White (BLANC), Dark Gray (3799), Sand (976), Black (310), Brown (434)
NOTIONS	Silver Thread	
	Black Wooden Bead (1, for the nose)	

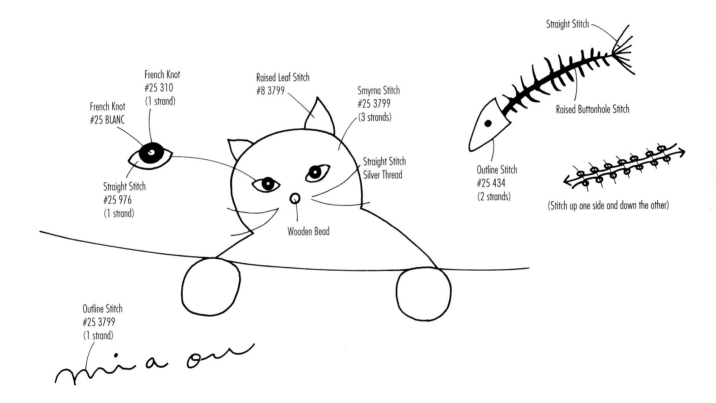

French Knot
#25 310
(1 strand)

French Knot
#25 BLANC

Raised Leaf Stitch
#8 3799

Smyrna Stitch
#25 3799
(3 strands)

Straight Stitch
#25 976
(1 strand)

Straight Stitch
Silver Thread

Wooden Bead

Outline Stitch
#25 3799
(1 strand)

Straight Stitch

Raised Buttonhole Stitch

Outline Stitch
#25 434
(2 strands)

(Stitch up one side and down the other)

Child's T-Shirt

shown on page 38

MATERIAL		Premade Child-sized T-shirt
THREADS	#8	Black (310)
	#25	White (BLANC), Black (310), Cream (3822)
NOTIONS		Silver Thread
		Wooden Bead (1, for the nose)

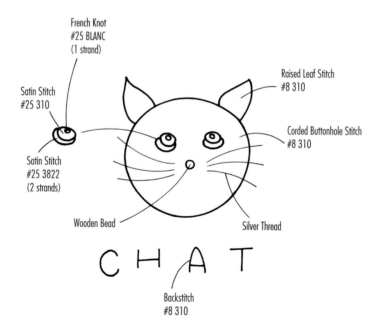

French Knot
#25 BLANC
(1 strand)

Satin Stitch
#25 310

Raised Leaf Stitch
#8 310

Corded Buttonhole Stitch
#8 310

Satin Stitch
#25 3822
(2 strands)

Wooden Bead

Silver Thread

Backstitch
#8 310

Adult-Sized T-Shirt shown on page 39

MATERIAL	Premade Adult-sized T-shirt	
THREADS	#8	Natural (840)
	#25	Brown (839)

Raised Buttonhole Stitch
#8 840

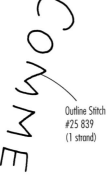

Outline Stitch
#25 839
(1 strand)

Coordinating Top and Skirt   shown on page 40

MATERIAL	Premade Skirt	
THREADS	#8	Chocolate Brown (898)
	#16	Coton à Broder (Anchor) White (1), Blue (976), Natural (387)
	#25	Black (310), Natural (ECRU)
NOTIONS	Felt (cut circles for corded buttonhole stitches)	
	Large Round Bead (1, for the nose)	

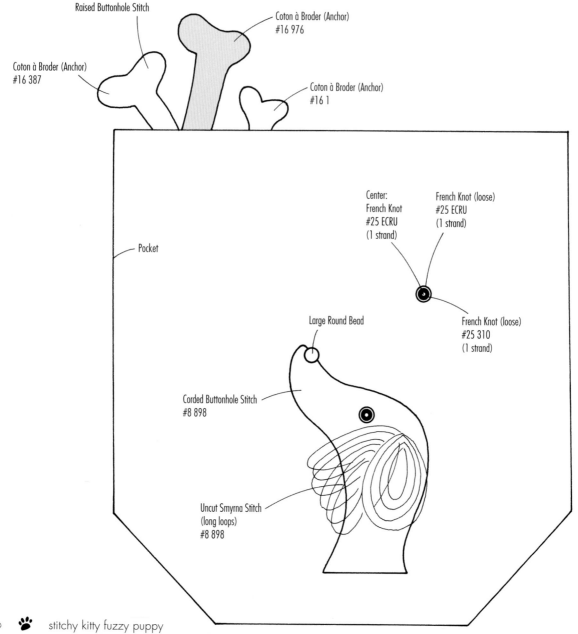

Raised Buttonhole Stitch

Coton à Broder (Anchor)
#16 976

Coton à Broder (Anchor)
#16 387

Coton à Broder (Anchor)
#16 1

Pocket

Center:
French Knot
#25 ECRU
(1 strand)

French Knot (loose)
#25 ECRU
(1 strand)

French Knot (loose)
#25 310
(1 strand)

Large Round Bead

Corded Buttonhole Stitch
#8 898

Uncut Smyrna Stitch
(long loops)
#8 898

MATERIAL	Premade Top
THREADS	#8 Red (817), White (BLANC), Dark Gray (3799)
	#25 Dark Gray (3799), Black (310), White (BLANC)
NOTIONS	Felt (cut circles for corded buttonhole stitches)

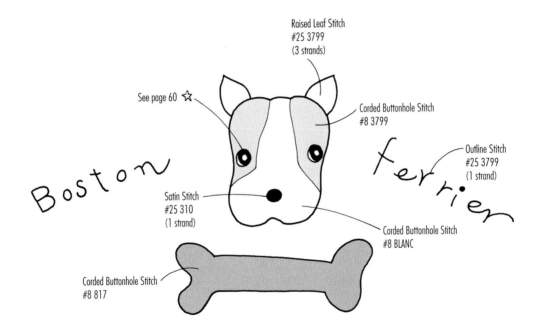

Raised Leaf Stitch
#25 3799
(3 strands)

See page 60 ☆

Corded Buttonhole Stitch
#8 3799

Outline Stitch
#25 3799
(1 strand)

Satin Stitch
#25 310
(1 strand)

Corded Buttonhole Stitch
#8 BLANC

Corded Buttonhole Stitch
#8 817

Boston terrier

One-Piece Dress shown on page 42

MATERIAL	Premade Dress	
THREADS	#8	White (BLANC), Dark Gray (3799), Brown (611)
	#25	Yellow (744), Green (3346), Dark Gray (3799), Natural (ECRU), Brown (729), Black (310), Red (817), White (BLANC)
NOTIONS	Black Wooden Bead (1, for the dog's nose)	
	Felt (cut circles for corded buttonhole stitches)	

Left side of pattern:

Backstitch
#8 3799

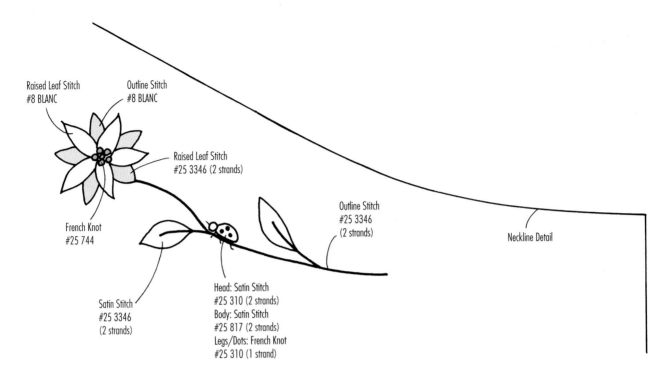

Raised Leaf Stitch
#8 BLANC

Outline Stitch
#8 BLANC

Raised Leaf Stitch
#25 3346 (2 strands)

French Knot
#25 744

Outline Stitch
#25 3346
(2 strands)

Neckline Detail

Satin Stitch
#25 3346
(2 strands)

Head: Satin Stitch
#25 310 (2 strands)
Body: Satin Stitch
#25 817 (2 strands)
Legs/Dots: French Knot
#25 310 (1 strand)

Right side of pattern:

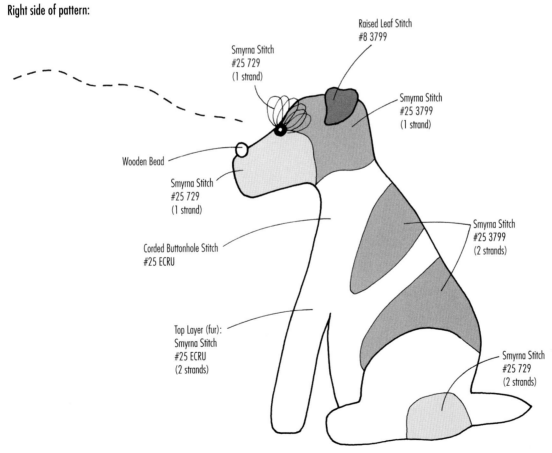

Smyrna Stitch
#25 729
(1 strand)

Raised Leaf Stitch
#8 3799

Smyrna Stitch
#25 3799
(1 strand)

Wooden Bead

Smyrna Stitch
#25 729
(1 strand)

Corded Buttonhole Stitch
#25 ECRU

Smyrna Stitch
#25 3799
(2 strands)

Top Layer (fur):
Smyrna Stitch
#25 ECRU
(2 strands)

Smyrna Stitch
#25 729
(2 strands)

Child's Hat and Bag Set   shown on page 43

MATERIAL	Premade Hat	
THREADS	#8	Natural (ECRU)
	#25	Black (310), Red (817), Green (3346), Pale Gray (413), Charcoal Gray (3371)

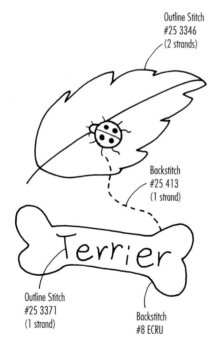

Outline Stitch
#25 3346
(2 strands)

Backstitch
#25 413
(1 strand)

Terrier

Outline Stitch
#25 3371
(1 strand)

Backstitch
#8 ECRU

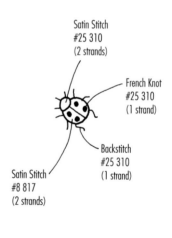

Satin Stitch
#25 310
(2 strands)

French Knot
#25 310
(1 strand)

Backstitch
#25 310
(1 strand)

Satin Stitch
#8 817
(2 strands)

MATERIAL	Premade Bag
THREADS	#8	Natural (ECRU), Pale Gray (413)
	#25	Black (310), Yellow (744), Green (3346), Natural (ECRU), Brown (420), Dark Gray (3799)
NOTIONS	Brown Wooden Bead (1, for the dog's nose)
	Felt (cut circles for corded buttonhole stitches)

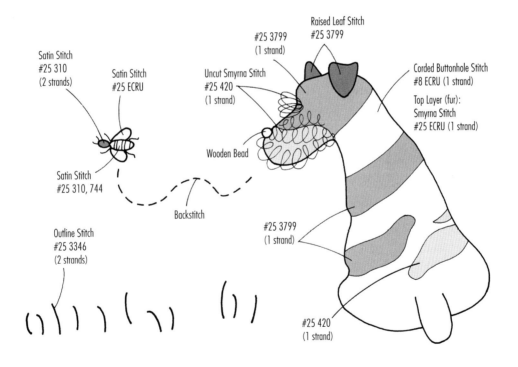

Satin Stitch
#25 310
(2 strands)

Satin Stitch
#25 ECRU

Satin Stitch
#25 310, 744

Outline Stitch
#25 3346
(2 strands)

Backstitch

Wooden Bead

Uncut Smyrna Stitch
#25 420
(1 strand)

#25 3799
(1 strand)

Raised Leaf Stitch
#25 3799

Corded Buttonhole Stitch
#8 ECRU (1 strand)

Top Layer (fur):
Smyrna Stitch
#25 ECRU (1 strand)

#25 3799
(1 strand)

#25 420
(1 strand)

Black Cat Hat and Scarf shown on page 44

MATERIALS	Premade Hat and Scarf	
THREADS	#8	Dark Brown (838), Brown (801), Black (310)
	Appleton	Brown (338)
NOTIONS	Wooden Bead (1, for the cat's nose)	

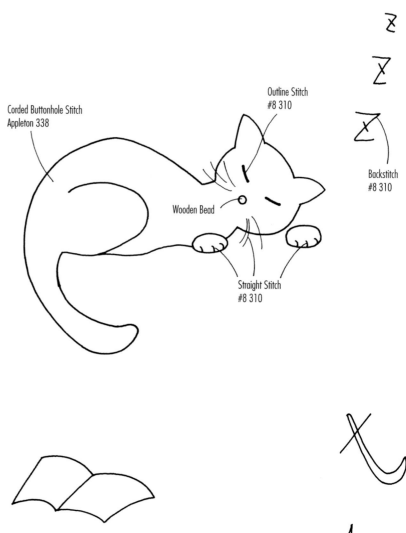

Corded Buttonhole Stitch
Appleton 338

Outline Stitch
#8 310

Wooden Bead

Backstitch
#8 310

Straight Stitch
#8 310

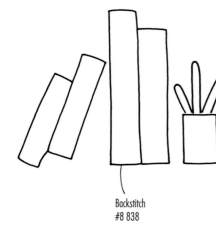

Backstitch
#8 838

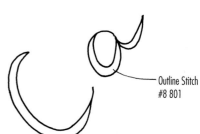

Outline Stitch
#8 801

Black Cat Mittens

shown on page 45

MATERIAL	Premade Mittens
THREADS	Appleton Black (993)

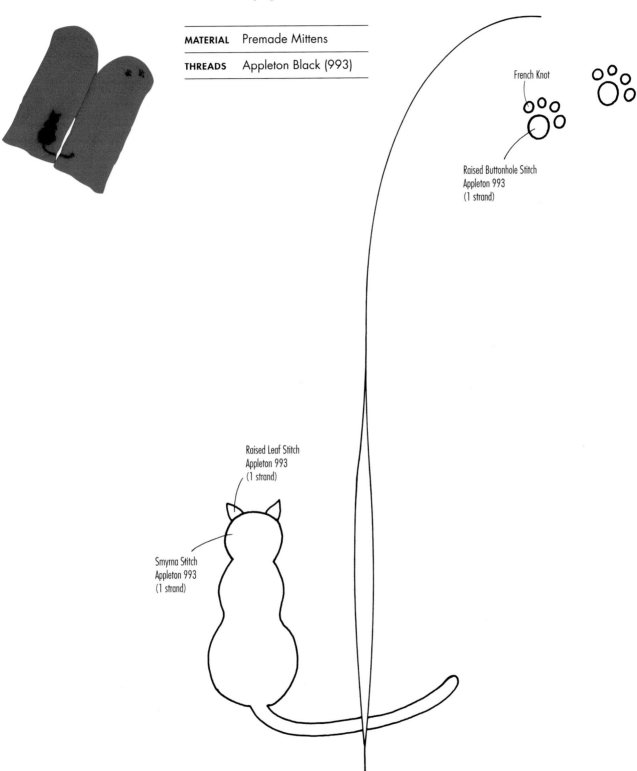

French Knot

Raised Buttonhole Stitch
Appleton 993
(1 strand)

Raised Leaf Stitch
Appleton 993
(1 strand)

Smyrna Stitch
Appleton 993
(1 strand)

Embroidery Thread Conversion Table

Use this table to find similar thread colors across three brands of floss—DMC, Anchor, and Cosmo.
Colors noted with a * may vary noticeably from the others.

DMC	ANCHOR	COSMO	DMC	ANCHOR	COSMO	DMC	ANCHOR	COSMO	DMC	ANCHOR	COSMO
301	1049	2129	611	898	*367	820	134	217	943	188	900
304	1006	241	702	226	273	825	*162	*255	946	332	*445
310	403	600	703	238	272	829	906	*775A	948	1011	340
318	*399	153A	729	890	575	831	*277	744	976	1001	129
321	9046	346	739	387	306	838	1088	*386	3032	831	366
350	11	344	740	316	147	839	1086	*2311	3033	391	364
356	5975	465	741	304	146	840	1084	384	3346	267	119
413	236	155	742	303	145	842	1080	*380	3371	382	312
414	*235	2154	743	302	144A	844	1041	*895	3781	904	369
420	374	575	744	301	143	898	360	2311	3799	236	*155
433	358	*309	781	308	706	900	333	758	3822	295	700
434	310	309	782	307	705A	907	*255	325A	3826	1049	2129
435	1046	308	783	306	703	918	341	*467	3859	*914	*463
437	362	*307	801	359	311	920	1004	188	BLANC	2	500
517	162	254	817	13	*346	938	381	2311	ECRU	387	305